Iona
of my
Heart

Iona of my Heart

of my

Daily readings

Neil Paynter (ed)

wild goose
publications

www.**iona**books.com

Published 2018 by
Wild Goose Publications
21 Carlton Court, Glasgow G5 9JP, UK,
the publishing division of the Iona Community.
Scottish Charity No. SC003794. Limited Company Reg. No. SC096243.

ISBN 978-1-84952-583-1

Cover photo © David Coleman

The publishers gratefully acknowledge the support of the Drummond Trust,
3 Pitt Terrace, Stirling FK8 2EY in producing this book.

Overseas distribution
Australia: Willow Connection Pty Ltd, Unit 4A, 3–9 Kenneth Road,
Manly Vale, NSW 2093
New Zealand: Pleroma, Higginson Street, Otane 4170, Central Hawkes Bay
Canada: Bayard Distribution, 10 Lower Spadina Ave., Suite 400, Toronto,
Ontario M5V 2Z

Printed by Bell & Bain, Thornliebank, Glasgow

In Iona of my heart, Iona of my love,
instead of monks' voices shall be the lowing of cattle;
but ere the world shall come to an end,
Iona shall be as it was.

– Gaelic prophecy attributed to Saint Columba

Time spent in community on Iona helps us to remember the sacrament of meals,
of voices raised in song and of stories shared from the heart.

– Fiona van Wissen, a guest on Iona in 2017

Introduction

The invitation to contribute to *Iona of My Heart* said:

> 'I'm looking for those *human* stories from Iona. You know
> the ones – we all have them. Stories about different folk
> coming together – people from different countries, back-
> grounds …
>
> Stories of encounter, challenge, exchange, connection,
> transformation …
>
> Stories about people and the power of the Spirit …
>
> *Show* why Iona and what the Iona Community does there
> is important to the world. Give it a human face …'

There's no inevitable, predictable Shakespeare or Samuel Johnson quote here. No Iona poems by people like Wordsworth, but stories, prayers and poems from folk like you and me, struggling to live and love today.

The royalties from *Iona of My Heart* will go to the Iona Community's Iona Abbey Capital Appeal (https://iona.org.uk/capital-appeal-information) and the Iona Community's work on Iona.

Thanks again to everyone who shared these pieces from the heart.

Neil Paynter, Christmas 2017

Month

Day 1

A sanctuary and a light

The Abbey community aims to be a group where people can feel safe – a sanctuary where they can open out, share their fears, reflect on their lives … Community life … grows fast as people wash dishes together, worship, engage in arts or music, and chat – at the dinner table, in the common room or Chapter House, on walks and out on the weekly pilgrimage round the island. During the course of the week people can expect to be affirmed – and challenged … Somehow, the Church at large must work at ways of restoring real community to its heart.

Ron Ferguson, a former Leader of the Iona Community, from Chasing the Wild Goose

O God, who gave to your servant Columba
the gifts of courage, faith and cheerfulness,
and sent people forth from Iona
to carry the word of your gospel to every creature:
grant, we pray, a like spirit to your church,
even at this present time.
Further in all things the purpose of our community,
that hidden things may be revealed to us,
and new ways found to touch the hearts of all.
May we preserve with each other
sincere charity and peace,
and if it be your will
grant that this place of your abiding be continued still
to be a sanctuary and a light.
Through Jesus Christ.
Amen

Prayer of the Iona Community

Day 2

Gary

A while back now, while I was chaplain at Red Tower Drug Rehab Centre in Helensburgh, Scotland, I encouraged several residents to have a week on Iona.

At the end of their stay, one of them, Gary, handed me this poem, which I thought was profound. The 'khaki hills' – a brilliant and precise description – were the hills along Loch Long, and the lamb 'just born, dappled mess' came into the world around Crianlarich.

I've no idea where Gary is now. He was around 19 then and the Centre is now closed. But I feel his poem lives on.

Fred Booth, a member of the Iona Community

The heavens rest on khaki hills
of heather, grass and daffodils.
Crying springs that rise to earth
will help to water her new birth.

A lamb, just born, dappled mess,
brings hope into the wilderness
of straying souls and weeping hearts
who ebb out as the sea departs.

They came, those saints from Ulster's shores,
to tell of Christ who, more and more,
gave of Himself till, cross held high,
that love which died for likes of I.

Then galleys came from Viking shores,
and Martyrs' Bay, once white, grew red.

And those who'd told of love on high
lay still on sand, all lifeless, dead.

I rest a while with praying thoughts
of what those Irish martyrs brought.
Did waters kindly lap their wounds
and take Christ's love to mainland ground?

And am I here travelling now
to sacred isle and healing days
because they gave, as their Christ gave,
the best they had for folk like me?

The heavens rest on khaki hills
of heather, grass and daffodils.
Crying springs that rise to earth
will help to water my new birth.

A lamb, just born, dappled mess,
brings hope into my wilderness.

From Coracle

Day 3

The journey begins

At last, after two changes, I was on the Glasgow to Oban train. I had heard
that this was a very beautiful run. And once the train began travelling
alongside Holy Loch onwards the view became increasingly breathtaking
– mountains, glens, lochs, forests and pure wilderness …

Then I was shocked to look down onto Faslane nuclear submarine base,
with its two enormous service sheds glimpsed through the trees. This feel-

ing was compounded as the train next passed into a small narrow glen which seemed full of nuclear storage bunkers. I counted 18, and it looked as if there were more further down the glen. It seemed to be truly a valley of death, in spite of its innocent tranquility. At that moment I felt called to pray silently as we passed these vaults of terrible destruction, as deeply as I could, that they would *never, never* be used either deliberately or accidently. I tried within my limited ability to bind the whole place within the *Light* of Christ.

A few miles further and the train came out high above another loch. Suddenly below us was a very wide rainbow, the widest I had ever seen. It stretched across the valley embracing the loch in God's sign of Peace. An answer to my prayers? I hoped so. I felt a deep sense of inner assurance that I had been heard, and my service as a volunteer at the Abbey had just begun …

Malcolm Whalan, an associate member of the Iona Community, who died in 2016

Day 4

'I'll pray for you': a week on Iona

The simple words 'I'll pray for you' can be hugely encouraging. Some years ago I organised a meeting of military generals, top civil servants and defence experts, coming together with assorted peace campaigners and church leaders for a week on Iona. At the start of the week I was understandably nervous, and a guest at the Abbey who was not a participant in the conference came up to me and said, 'Would you like me to pray for you all during the conference?' I accepted her offer, rather with the attitude of, *Oh well, if she would like to do that it can't do any harm.*

From time to time throughout the week we would meet in passing and she would simply give me a little nod of acknowledgement. Gradually I realised that the knowledge of her prayerful support was becoming more and more significant. By the end of a truly amazing week, I realised just how important her prayers had been. It was not just that I personally felt calmed and supported by her thoughts; it was also a tapping into some kind of intangible energy that could be felt at our meetings. I think we were all surprised, and one of the military men summed it up with his parting words as he stepped onto the ferry: 'Only the hand of God could have dumped me into the midst of a bunch of raving peace women!' Then he looked me directly in the eye and said, 'And I mean it.'[1]

Helen Steven, a member of the Iona Community, who died in 2016, from No Extraordinary Power

1. From *No Extraordinary Power: Prayer, Stillness and Activism*, Helen Steven, Quaker Books, 2005. Used by permission of Quaker Books.

Day 5

The low door

Not long after we arrived last weekend I turned at the bottom of the stone steps from the Abbey refectory and walked into the common room, literally *into* the common room – banging my head against the door frame, forgetting, as I do every May at this time, how much shorter people were then. This is the time of year when I crack my head.

I did it again on Tuesday, coming out of that miniature shop with a miniature door behind the Columba Hotel. The one called 'The Low Door', which has a sign that reads 'Please Mind Your Head. Beware of the Low Door' that you notice just after you've walked into it.

We were pregnant when we first made the journey to Iona. That was an entire family ago now. We kept returning, with more and more children, climbing up through England, leaving the city behind, except the cities we carry inside us. 'I want to take it all in,' is how Meg puts it on the way, transfixed by forest and loch through the train window, lighthouse and castle from the ferry deck. 'Usually,' she says, 'you want a journey to end.'

My case must seem large for a week away. 'Mart?' says Rhi, 'that's a lot of luggage you've got there.' I wanted to explain that holdalls and suitcases, rucksacks and bags are not always what they seem. How they carry a library of fiction and poetry. That I think of a suitcase as an analogue Kindle. But maybe I'd been packing for the kids too. The ones who aren't with us this time. The ones who came with us, the first time, an entire family ago.

We met Duncan on the machair, bending down to retrieve a lost golf ball. He'd broken his oatcake with me after the Sunday service. I remembered him from last year, same time, same place. In the meantime, I'd met his daughters, who turned up at our church in north London. We discovered we'd been meeting their aunt, Duncan's sister, Helen, on this week for twenty years. Watched her children grow and she ours.

One morning, the Bard of Lewis, Alastair McIntosh, told us that Iona was once the centre of an ancient 'information superhighway'. It's still an original meeting place. Duncan said his family have been coming here since 1965. His parents met here in 1938, not long after George MacLeod brought Columba over from Ireland.

That bay where he first landed, bent down to touch the ground, was where we stopped on our Tuesday pilgrimage; and Pete invited us to think of some burden in our lives we wanted to get rid of … and then to pick up a pebble and throw it in the sea. I got stuck, I always do, but settled for greed and fell in step down to the shore with Rufus, a 10-year-old boy, whose arms clutched to his chest a great green boulder. 'That's a big burden,' I said, bending low to talk. 'What are you getting rid of?' 'My brother,' he said. 'He's *so* annoying.'

In the Abbey we light candles for our friends, the ones for whom words are long past their sell-by, and for whom we long now only for poetry and light. In the morning service we remembered the people shot dead in Belgium, and in the U.S., and their loved ones, Iona being one of the rare places where breaking news comes in the intercessions.

That information superhighway may be ancient, while most days the 21st-century one is not available. Which is why I'm sitting high in the Abbey library now, once again, leaning out the window, stretching my hand into the sky, holding out my phone in supplication for my e-mails. Only to find repeated the solemn response, 'Your connection to the server has failed.'

But the connection has never failed here in all these years. Tenderly I touch the top of my head and remind myself again to bow down in this place, and of how you need to bow down in any place to notice you are on holy ground; and that's why we come here maybe: to remind ourselves that *all ground* is holy ground, and we are *'here to kneel'*.*

Martin Wroe, an associate of the Iona Community

* T.S. Eliot, from 'Little Gidding'

Day 6

Columba's Shrine

Your narrow door is always open.
Your chairs always ready for conversation.
Or silence.
Your rich carpet ready to receive
the feet of the curious tourist,
or the prostrate form of the penitent.

I came with heavier burdens than I realised.
A broken marriage I thought I had processed.
A court date for careless driving
when I returned home.
Mounting financial bills.
Could I afford to be here?
Did I deserve to be here?

I was not ready
to give up my burdens
in the community worship that first night.

Saint Columba,
Tame the water beasts below my conscious mind.
Take my restless heart,
tossing as a coracle on the sea,
and pray for me.
Through Christ,
the Calmer of Storms, I pray.

Leaving my burdens at the Shrine's altar
I turn toward the saint's portal.
My stomach already quieter,
my shoulders already lighter,
I step out into the Abbey's night
and smile at the stars …

And they sing back.

Mark A. Smith

Day 7

The power at work among us

It was Friday lunch, a time for staff to relax together and eat up leftovers from recent meals at the Centres. At the MacLeod Centre, we had just said goodbye to a group of refugees and community workers who spent the week with us. It had been a moving week. One of the families was called back early to face a hearing on their right to remain in Britain. When I said goodbye to them at the ferry, they embraced me with tears in their eyes. 'This is the first time we felt welcome since we arrived in Britain,' they told me. Humbling words to pass along to my colleagues on staff.

At the lunch table, I was joined by a young man volunteering with us for a few weeks. Normally a cheerful lad with a scheme or two up his sleeve, he looked solemn. 'Do you ken what those people have been through, Nancy? It's just nae fair.' He had been deeply moved by what he'd heard from our guests.

I reflected on the power at work among us. This young man had come to get his life straightened out. He'd had a brush with the law. Someone in the Iona Community's network thought time on Iona would help him make a fresh start. In lots of ways, he hadn't had a fair chance either. Yet here he was, marvelling at the courage of refugees also trying to make a fresh start. Their stories lay beyond anything he could imagine, just as his story lay beyond my experience.

Nancy Cocks, a former Director of the MacLeod Centre, from Invisible We See You

The upside-down life of the Kingdom

Dealing with Saturday arrivals was always a bit tricky. Most folk arrive in the early afternoon, others in ones and twos later on. Still others, taking the last ferry, arrive after 6:00 and join supper late. All arrive tired and hungry. So supper on Saturday evenings is a challenge: both to feed bodies and to form community.

It was baked potatoes that evening, with a variety of fillings, but they were not ready – you can imagine that 70 potatoes take a lot of baking! So, we sang a song, did the notices, introduced ourselves … and still they weren't ready …

Finally, one of my colleagues made the out of the box suggestion that we should have our pudding first. So – with much laughter – we did! Apple crumble and custard, followed by baked potatoes, beans and cheese. Such is the upside-down life of the Kingdom!

Richard Sharples, a former Iona Abbey Warden

A place where the labels are off

'When you get off the boat onto Iona, the labels are off. And when you get back to Glasgow, they go on again.'

Perceptive musings from Celia, a member of Glasgow Braendam Link (GBL), after a week at the MacLeod Centre.

GBL works in partnership with families in Glasgow living in poverty and social exclusion, with the purpose of encouraging them to speak out and be heard – about *their* lives. They, after all, are the experts.

'The worst thing of all – worse than being poor, living in bad areas, having to choose between heating the house and eating dinner, all these things – is to know that you count for nothing.'

The annual Iona visits were memorable in so many ways.

So many 'firsts'. Out of Glasgow, the journey, meals prepared for you, and sitting at a table to eat them, beautiful beaches, meaningful worship, not being judged, feeling part of the whole set-up …

Betty helped serve Communion; Cathy (overweight) climbed Dun I – and felt she'd conquered the world; children thrived in their own programme; other guests, the Resident group and vollies listened to folk's stories, and were deeply moved.

At the end of week assessment session, GBL members, over and over again, would say what a great thing it had been for them to serve the meals and do the chores with all these really 'important' people, like teachers, doctors, social workers, knowing each other on first name terms, and not being judged or written off as failures, as they were so used to.

But the really exciting thing was the response from the 'important' people. 'Well,' they so often said, 'this has been a very special time for us. We don't often have a chance to meet people who are struggling in their lives, except in a professional capacity, and this week we've got to know you as real people, and that's been very special for us.'

There are not many places where the labels are off in this unique way. Our task is to ensure they are always off in our Centres, and to find ways of keeping them off in all our places of work and being.

Molly Harvey, a member of the Iona Community

Day 10

A place where I felt whole again

I first came to Iona when I was 19 and in second-year university. Iona scared me initially. Being trapped on a small island for any amount of time made me feel lightheaded and dizzy. Most of all, the thought of being trapped there with Christians made me want to run in the opposite direction! Yet that week was transformative for me. I met Christians from around the world, and I was humbled as I listened to people's stories which showed how faith was alive and active for them. It made me think, question and wonder.

I struggle with prayer, and always will, yet the daily Iona services offered steadiness, enabling me to feel God for the first time. I could feel God's power and might in the Abbey as we prayed as a collective, emphasising once more what I already knew: that humans were not meant to live alone – we are called to be in community. On Iona that seemed more obvious than ever, and it left me with the challenge of how to continue to develop places of community in my future.

The second time I came to Iona I was 22 years old. I was simply broken. I have rheumatoid arthritis and had experienced a couple of bad years with it. I arrived with the knowledge that walking would be difficult and the long walks I enjoyed on my previous visit were no longer an option. I had come knowing I needed a wheelchair, but not bringing one, partly out of stubbornness.

The Iona Community saw my disability, yet *did not* see or define me by it. They introduced me to a lovely Liverpudlian Iona Community member, David Horton, who organised a scooter for me to use when I wished. David saw past the scooter and my obvious brokenness and offered friendship and care. His attitude rubbed off on my fellow travellers. Gone were the kid gloves they had unknowingly worn and I had unknowingly accepted. Iona became a place where I could be in a scooter but not *feel* in a scooter. Iona and its community members healed me, not physically, but emotionally. Iona was where I felt whole again, and that feeling has never left me.

I am returning this summer (2016), without need of a scooter, as a volunteer. I will always be thankful to the community that made me feel whole, taught me about community and enabled me to feel God in prayer for the first time.

Laura Wood, Youth and children's worker

Day 11

'You get to start over'

We arrived just before 10:00am. I can be such a pain when it comes to not being on time that I'm sure my husband rolls his eyes a lot! But we got there. We were in Philadelphia and were attending worship with the Beacon Community, who identify themselves as a neighbourhood faith community that invites people of all ages to grow together through the arts, learning and faith. Once a month the community gathers for worship, and I had planned our time in Philadelphia specifically around their worship schedule. I had met the co-directors at a conference earlier in the year and was fascinated by their story of resurrection in what had been an 'inherited' church. So in mid-July, Nick and I travelled to Philly as part of my sabbatical.

Worship with that community was the kind of occasion that theologian Frederick Buechner says to pay attention to. There was just something about worshipping with that group that got to me – it was the most real, most authentic worship I had been part of in quite some time, and my tears flowed freely in the midst of the service. There was no pretense. There was no 'this is what church ought to be'. There was an honesty in their presence and practice that caught me short. It was not until later in my sabbatical that I began to understand what had happened.

The later came during my week on Iona. I attended a week led by the Wild Goose Resource Group: 'What is this place? Who are these people?' It was a week of exploration of looking at the places where we worship in order to make them more appropriate and responsive for use, and at the people who gather in them, and whether what happens in the spaces speaks to and for them. That was the 'official' description, but it was so much more than that for me, and it started on the Sunday afternoon.

Our first gathering was with Graham Maule and it was a 'mapping' exercise. I had never done one of these before and was a bit confused before even entering the room. And then Graham started in with what maps did, how they functioned, etc. 'Now,' he said, 'I want you to map an event in your life, or map the sounds of the birds, or map the movement of the cows …' (OK, he didn't say that last one but might as well have for all the clarity this gave me!). My confusion only deepened. I had no idea what he was talking about. I need some help with this, I thought. And as though he was reading my mind, he said, 'And if you need some help, I have a bowl of random words, and you can choose one of these to get you started.' Well, I might as well, I thought, because nothing else was helping. I reached into the bowl and chose the word 'forgotten'. Armed with a piece of paper, two coloured pens and a random word, I planted myself on a bench outside to reflect upon what I had 'forgotten' – I had forgotten keys, phone numbers, people's names … what else? And then in a voice as clear as day I heard, *'You have forgotten me.'* I looked around to see if anyone else had heard it, but no one else seemed to have. Then I thought: Well, I must be daydreaming, because I'm Presbyterian and we just don't hear voices. And yet, it was so very real and so very true: I had forgotten God.

I was so very tired when I'd left for my sabbatical. I was tired of day-to-day minutiae. I was tired of the building issues. I was tired of writing sermons. I was tired of putting together church bulletins. I was tired, tired, tired. And one of the reasons why is because I had forgotten. I had forgotten that I was not in this all on my own. I had forgotten that God had called me. I had forgotten to claim God's grace. I had forgotten God's timing. I had forgotten God's purpose. I had forgotten God's invitation. Quickly, I drew 'A map of forgotten things'.

And then, throughout the week, I was invited to remember. Through music, liturgy, worship, conversation and prayer, I was invited to remember.

The next day, we had a 'space' experience. It was a 'strange' experience in that the room had been darkened. There were sheets of paper hanging. Sand was thrown on the floor; crockery was crushed; light bounced around and changed colours; sounds bounced off the wall. And then it all *stopped*! The shades on the windows were removed and all the stuff (junk really) that had ended up on the floor was carted away. The room was bare – with the light streaming in. Then a white cloth was laid on the floor; small tables were brought in and bowls of water placed on them. Grapes and daisies appeared, and we shared them with one another. Tears were streaming down my face – what the heck is going on here?! And then the voice, not as loud as before, but present nonetheless: *'You get to start over.'* All the crap, all the minutiae, all the stuff – it is hauled away, and you get to start over.

The tears at Beacon and the tears on Iona at the sight of the white cloth and light were strangely similar. No stuff, no crap, no minutiae – just all that is important, all that is real, all that God calls me to.

I get to start over.

Sharon Core

Day 12

Engagement rather than escape

What brings so many people to Iona is essentially a spiritual journey in search of meaning, purpose and value at a time when so many of the old certainties seem to be breaking down, exposed as inadequate to the tensions, questions and pressures of today, and traditional institutions, the church included, do not fully meet people's needs. 'Celtic spirituality' in particular has a fascination, a curiosity value and attraction because of its perceived association with remote natural beauty and the past, and is often explored in the context of the quest for personal growth that reflects the current individualistic ethos. The Iona Community's understanding of spirituality, however, has to do with engagement rather than the kind of escape that smacks of nostalgia and the romantic. It is founded on the incarnational theology that has characterised the life of the Community since its outset. It asserts that the genuine Celtic tradition of spirituality, as found in the Columban church, had a strong social and communal dimension: God is thoroughly down-to-earth, to be discovered, encountered and experienced not only in personal reflective meditation but also in the practicalities and particularities of life, in human struggles and relationships as much as in tranquility and the contemplation of natural beauty. *'Spirituality is where prayer and politics meet,'* as Kate McIlhagga, a Community member, said.

Norman Shanks, a former Leader of the Iona Community, from Chasing the Wild Goose

Day 13

'The likes of me'

For some years on Iona we hosted, each summer, a group who stayed for two weeks in the youth camp, and came from the Six Circle movement. This movement was the brainchild of a remarkable Governor of Polmont Borstal. He had felt that young people with challenging situations could find help from other young people in similar circumstances. So he had started this organisation, and each year came to Iona with some young people from the borstal, others in the care of the nearby social work department, and yet others who were cerebral palsy patients from the local Larbert Hospital.

As you can imagine, putting all these different groups together under one roof on Iona presented considerable challenges. But, as is often the case on Iona, the place, and the context of the life together, worked its healing work, and these lads who had begun the holiday very suspicious of each other usually ended it by becoming fast friends.

Two particular events stand out for me about these camps. On the pilgrimage day on the second week of one of them, we were all gathered outside the Abbey to start, waiting for the young people from the youth camp. When eventually they appeared, to our amazement the boys from the borstal came down carrying the boys from Larbert Hospital on sedan chairs, which the borstal boys had manufactured, by themselves, from broom handles and chairs from the Abbey church. And these lads carried the Larbert boys all the way round the pilgrimage route without a word of complaint – at least, none I heard – including all the way up Dun I and back down again!

Then, on the last night of one of the Six Circle camps, we were gathered in the Abbey church for the usual Friday night communion. One of the leaders of the group, I remember, was a blind social worker – so when we sang

'Amazing Grace' – 'I once was blind, but now I see' – there were, as you can imagine, tears aplenty. As we always do, we passed the peace, shaking each other's hands. After the service was over, I was the last out of the church – and when I came into the darkened cloisters, I heard what sounded like someone crying over in a corner. When I went across, I found one of the boys from the borstal, in tears. Thinking he was upset at having to go back to borstal the next day, I started to try to comfort him. 'No,' he sobbed, 'it's not that. It's I never thought anyone would want to shake hands with the likes of me, in a church.'

John Harvey, a former Iona Abbey Warden and Leader of the Iona Community

Day 14

A place at the table

I travelled to Iona for the first time in 2006 to join an LGBT week. On the boat from Oban to Mull I was wondering which of all the passengers were going to Iona for the LGBT week too. While waiting for the ferry at Fionnphort I spoke to a man, who asked me if I was a guest for the Abbey or the MacLeod Centre. I told him I was coming for the LGBT week in the Mac: my first 'coming out' that day, and it felt very comfortable. This man told me he was a minister of a church in the U.S. and remarked that the church had not always been kind to the gay community. His statement – that it was all right to be gay and a Christian – healed my soul. I had recently had my 'coming out' with my home church in the Netherlands, which had been very difficult.

On the way from the jetty to the Mac I walked along with Grace, and we had a nice chat. Throughout the week we met one another several times and checked that we were both all right and enjoying ourselves. I remember Grace with affection.

Our group was involved in the Thursday evening Communion, which somehow became a very 'pink' service. Gathered in the Abbey nave, with the rainbow flag spread out from where communion was served, it was beautiful to experience everyone together in unity. We sang the song 'For everyone born, a place at the table', by Shirley Erena Murray.

After all these experiences, I could not sleep at night, and dreamt of the possibility of a 'pink service' in my home church.

Since the Iona week I have changed to a more ecumenical church where being gay is no problem; and since 2009 have helped organise a 'pink service' there once a year.

The Iona Community, the Dutch Iona Group and my home church have helped me greatly to accept that I am a lesbian and that it is all right to be so – and certainly not a problem for God.

Annie Benjamin, a member of the Dutch Iona Group

Day 13

A story of hope

Immediately following the first Gulf War, an interfaith conference was held on the holy isle of Iona. From this, a joint Muslim-Christian communiqué resulted in the decision that national interfaith services of reconciliation would take place. One would be in Edinburgh's St Giles' Cathedral and the other in Glasgow Mosque.

But a problem arose with the Edinburgh event. The timing was going to clash with the Muslims' evening call to prayer. They would be unable to attend. It was then that Dr Bashir Maan, the spokesperson for Glasgow Mosque, remembered something from the Hadith, the oral tradition of

Islam. Seemingly Prophet Mohammed (peace be upon him) had allowed visiting Christians to use his mosque for their worship. Might it be conceivable, he wondered, for us likewise to do something in this spirit?

Scotland's Christian leaders responded warmly. They would even allow Muslim worship to be conducted in front of the altar at St Giles' Cathedral as part of the service. So it came to pass that Christians watched on as Muslims prayed in their church. Our silence felt respectful to the point of inner participation.

The following week, on 25 October 1991, Imam Tufail Hussain Shah addressed Christians at prayer in the community hall of the Glasgow Mosque. Referring to the previous week's event, he said, '*We joined that night, and again now in this mosque, to worship the same God. God as known to the early Jews as Yahweh. God as revealed in the Christian tradition through Jesus Christ. God whom we Muslims know by the Arabic word Allah … We share a common commitment to love, justice, charity, mercy, piety and peace. Building these qualities in our hearts perhaps matters more to God than cleverness in arguing about religion. I believe it is God, Allah, who has brought us together. Let us try to stay together and work for peace not only in the Gulf and Middle East, but throughout this planet, this universe of God.*'

Some years later I was telling this story whilst lecturing in Edinburgh University. The son of a Nigerian imam came up to me afterwards. 'You know,' he told me, 'we read all about that in our newspaper in Nigeria.' He explained to me that at the time Muslims and Christians were killing each other in his country. His father and his colleagues were so astonished to hear that Scottish Christians could talk with Muslims that they decided to initiate the same approach with Christian leaders in their area. The killings did not entirely stop as a result, but they greatly reduced.

Alastair McIntosh, an associate of the Iona Community

Day 16

Litany of celebration (written for a service in Iona Abbey)

Dear God, we thank you for
the richness, gifts and contributions
of different cultures

We thank you for:

Nelson Mandela
Archbishop Desmond Tutu
Rosa Parks
Mahatma Gandhi

For Ray Charles singing 'Georgia' and
Little Richard singing 'Tutti Frutti, oh rutti'

For the vocal harmonies of Ladysmith Black Mambazo

For Boogie woogie
Bebop
Jazz
Rap
Funk
Soul
Rock 'n' roll

Salsa clubs
The samba
Spirituals and voices
deep and profound as wells of living water

For the heady smell of the Indian grocers
For cardamom, saffron, cloves
jasmine, patchouli, sandalwood

For the music of accents
dance of gestures
communication of smiles

For the lined landscapes of beautiful faces

For kebabs
hummus
baklava
goulash
won ton soup
warm naan bread
tandoori
sweet and sour
rice and peas and curried goat

For Greek delicatessens
Arabic delicatessens
Italian delicatessens
For delicatessens!

For gold jewellery against black skin
the sound of reggae from the car repair shop
the pungent, sour smell of indigo-dyed cloth
the blast and blare of Notting Hill Carnival.

Neil Paynter and others

Day 17

Light shining

People travel great distances to find holiness. Some even come to Iona.

Here is a little story I heard from somewhere, years ago …

A boy lived in an isolated house on a hill. A godforsaken place for a young man. But one thing fascinated him. Each night he would look out into the darkness and see a light. It was far away on a hilltop, but this sign of life gave him hope.

One day he decided to go in search of it. It was a long and lonely walk, and it was already dark before he reached the outskirts of a town. Tired and hungry, he knocked at the first door he came to, and explained his search for the mysterious light that had always given him hope.

'I know it!' replied the woman who had answered the door. 'It gives me hope as well.' And she pointed back in the direction from which he had come.

There, on the horizon, was a single light shining. A sign of life in the darkness.

The light from his house.

Brian Woodcock, a former Iona Abbey Warden, from Advent Readings from Iona

Day 18

'The strength to carry on': Priority Areas Holiday Week on Iona

When the sun shines, Iona is one of the most beautiful places on the planet – and even when the rain is battering down it is still pretty stunning. During Priority Areas Holiday Week one July we had a mixture of both – thankfully more of the former than the latter – but whatever the weather, this was a truly unforgettable week.

First and foremost it was a holiday: a welcome break for young and old from some of our very poorest neighbourhoods in Scotland. And so there were lots of visits to the beaches, when the sun came out. There was a spectacular water slide – in the front garden of Dunsmeorach – that must have had the day tourists open-mouthed with amazement (and, I suspect, George MacLeod birling in his grave). And there was an evening of pampering for the grown-ups: manicure, massage, great food and deep relaxation.

For holidaymakers this was also a time for faith to be stretched and nurtured. I personally don't think that you can be on Iona without that happening. For some, that was in the Abbey church, as we joined pilgrims from across the world in a building and in words which have inspired generations. For others, it took place in our specially crafted 'Worship in the wild'. This was worship which sought to provide a window of faith for the many who experience God every day, but feel that they don't necessarily belong in the church.

One of my personal highlights was taking wee groups of young people up the 'mountain of Dun I' – and just watching their sense of wonder as they scrambled up to the cairn on the top and gazed in every direction. And the trip to Staffa was incredible. Forget the seals basking on the rocks, the puffins almost eating out of folk's hands and the dolphins dancing along after the boat. The real high (and low) point was travelling back on a vessel that felt like a roller coaster as we were tossed about from side to side and up and down! Many of us arrived at the jetty very wet and exceptionally green!

The image of being 'tossed about from side to side' is worth sticking with. Many of those on the holiday had gone through tough times, and are still doing so. Priority Areas is how the Church of Scotland describes the very poorest parishes in Scotland. Although these are wonderful places full of amazing people, the struggle against poverty is part of many people's everyday life and never far from the surface. Iona was an amazing place for us to spend a holiday, and I want to offer a huge thanks to members of the Iona Community for their generosity in helping to make this possible.

After a previous Priority Areas holiday one mum told me how the week on Iona gave her and her family 'the strength to carry on', to live on the memories of not just the views but, more importantly, the friendships and the sense of being cared about. One wee lad told me that it was the 'best week of his life'. One dad, who had been really fearful about coming, on the second day was running joyfully about the beach being chased by children with buckets full of water. Lots of families went home with videos of corncrakes on their mobile phones. One friend talked about how he was returning home having enjoyed three meals a day, and was determined to maintain that pattern back in Glasgow. And the friendships which were made on Iona will last a lifetime.

However, the Priority Areas Week is not just of immense value to the holidaymakers, although it is most certainly that; it is also a wonderful opportunity to practise and demonstrate courageous hospitality. The Priority Areas Holiday Week is special because both centres (and Camas) are filled to capacity with people from many of Scotland's very poorest neighbourhoods. That brings its challenges – and we experienced a few of those – but it also brings huge rewards and insight. In my experience, it brings us close to the Gospel and to God's special passion and compassion for those who struggle against the grind of poverty, day in and day out. I wouldn't have missed it for the world.

Martin Johnstone, from Coracle

Martin Johnstone is a founding director of Faith in Community Scotland and is an associate of the Iona Community. For fifteen years, he was the Church of Scotland's Priority Areas Secretary.

Day 19

Robert and Salah: 'a bit of Iona'

One of the most satisfying things that I did as a student chaplain in Glasgow was to take groups of international students to Iona. You spend a lot of time trying to persuade them to go. And it's after a few days there that they say to you, 'Why didn't you tell us it was going to be like this?!'

Two folk particularly stand out amongst those who were to have the Iona Community experience. Robert was still in his teens. He had escaped from Rhodesia to Malawi, where Iona Community member and veteran missionary in Africa Tom Colvin was busy getting passports for those fleeing white domination and sending them on to Scotland. The first port of call was Community House in Glasgow, where Community member Malcolm May was Deputy Warden. He phoned me to investigate accommodation, and within a few days Robert was staying with compatriots and on a nurse training course.

On Iona he quickly adjusted to the Abbey camp experience into which he threw himself – and the following year there was no difficulty in persuading him to help lead a week's camp on the island on his holiday from nursing.

Salah was from Alexandria in Egypt. His course seemed to be well set towards a BSC in engineering at Glasgow University, before returning home. He was quiet, but enthusiastic about joining in with the variety of social events that the chaplaincy promoted. A week on Iona was one such and he attended everything on the programme, including Abbey worship. The experience meant so much to him that he signed up for a second student week the following year.

Robert returned to Zimbabwe, having qualified as an accountant, but resigned from a government post after he resisted political pressure to sacrifice his integrity. Since then he has exercised a distinguished ministry in north and south London Methodist circuits. Attending one of his services I noticed a familiar nuance to part of the worship and told him. 'Oh yes, that's a bit of Iona,' he said with a laugh.

Salah for some years has been spokesman for the Muslim Council of Scotland, bringing wisdom to broadcasts and statements on the crucial issues faced by Islam and being committed to interfaith understanding and peace, as is the Iona Community.

Iain Whyte, a member of the Iona Community

Day 20

An ocean of tears

Among the most sought-after pebbles along the shorelines of Iona is the nephrite, a small green stone lodged in Ionan marble, gradually released by the tides. Most people call these prized finds 'Columba's tears', connecting their shape and existence with the grief Saint Columba experienced when he left his native Ireland behind for good and landed on Iona for the first time.

You can't find such precious stones right away. You have to sit in one spot for a while at Columba's Bay, digging and sifting, pushing away layers of other stones little by little until, maybe, if you're lucky, a tear emerges. They say only one person per group of pilgrims goes home with this treasure; it wasn't me.

I did discover other tears: my own.

During a prayer walk around the Abbey one morning, our pilgrimage leader invited us to be still for ten minutes, in a place of our own choosing. I was drawn to the Quiet Corner, where worshippers can pray in semi-privacy. The light of a small window caught my attention. I pulled up a little bench and looked out onto the lush grass that surrounds the Abbey's walls.

Less than a minute of silence passed before I heard the voices of little children playing on the other side of the glass. In the mystery of that moment, their gleeful voices rang out like a call to prayer.

As I watched and listened, I remembered the words from the service of baptism of the French Reformed Church, which are framed on the wall of my bedroom:

Little child,
for you Christ came.
He struggled, he suffered.
For you he endured the darkness of Gethsemane
and the agony of Calvary.
For you he triumphed over death,
and you, little child,
know nothing of all this …

Did the little children through my window know anything about Christ's love for them? If not, his love was still there, reaching out with gentle but persistent generosity.

I started to cry, unexpectedly overwhelmed by God's boundless embrace of these young souls – and of all the world's children.

I thought of my own nineteen-year-old child, at whose baptism the pastor invoked those words from the French Reformed Church, now miles away from the Iona Community in basic training for the U.S. Army. He and I both tenderly acknowledge that 'infantry is not my first choice' for him. Yet gazing through the pane I saw in newly illumined ways that God's heart transcends and enfolds any human choice, including his – and mine.

I thought of my mother, slipping behind dementia's curtain, emerging every so often with a memory, an astute comment, a strong opinion, or my name. She knows me. But what does she know today of Christ's abundance? At eighty-six she may know nothing of it; yet he loves her still.

I took a deep breath and slowly turned my gaze inward. Twenty-three years in ministry, and yet the astonishing possibility that I, too, could be encompassed by such boundless grace washed over me as if for the first time.

I didn't travel to Iona intending to uncover an ocean of tears. But as the children's voices faded and our group resumed the prayer walk, I carried their release like a treasure. I always will.

Susan E. Steinberg

Day 21

A prayer of thanksgiving for the common life on Iona

Written for a service of thanksgiving in Iona Abbey

Loving God, we thank you for the sounds of the common life:
the swish and the scrub,
the plane and the polish,
the click and the conversation,
the ring and the riotous laughter,
the song and the silence.
May you encircle us with the sounds of your community.

Loving God, we thank you for the smells of the common life:
the freshly laundered linen,
the compost heap,
the damp and sweat of pilgrimage day,
the sweet and savoury of mealtimes and kitchens,
the pungent mingling of scents in the herb garden.
May you envelop us with the fragrance of your love among us.

Loving God, we thank you for the taste of the common life:
the wonderful simplicity of soup and bread,
salads and roast dinners,
great trays of bakes,
the signs of your creative glory
in chocolate-puddle pudding and raspberry roulade.
May you nourish us with your grace in sharing.

Loving God, we thank you for the touch of the common life:
the keyboard and keypad,
first-aid phone and flapjack,

candles and cushions,
spanners and spades,
kayak and cleaning cloth,
boxes of books
and children glorying in glue and games.
May you enfold us in the warmth of your restful embrace.

And we thank you for the staff and volunteers here
in this time and place.
May they know your love and pleasure
in their commitment to the common life.
And for all who live on this island,
working to offer hospitality and refreshment,
we give you thanks.

Alison Swinfen, a member of the Iona Community, from Coracle

Day 22

An invitation to the Great Feast

Young folk from Bellahouston Academy have been coming to Iona for over 25 years, and Iona Community youth workers past and present have done wonderful creative work with them at their school in the south side of Glasgow.

During a week on Iona in 2012, pupils from Bellahouston – besides having a brilliant time down on the north beach, enjoying a boat trip to Staffa, and dancing at the ceilidh in the village hall – looked at different world issues in their daily reflection sessions. In one they looked at the culture and peoples of Mexico, and liberation theology, which, they discovered, had come out of the political struggles of the poor in Latin America and is about 'seeing society through the eyes of the marginalised'.

With great care and passion – and excitement – the young people created a worship service inspired by these ideas, and by Luke 14:15–24 – the parable of the Great Feast.

Towards the end of worship they invited everyone in the Abbey to come and share in a great party! Folk were invited to write the names of people or groups they viewed as excluded or ostracised from society on invitations left by their seats, and to come to the table in the crossing – which was decorated with balloons – and to place their invitation on the table: to include these folk in the feast of life. 'The table represents the radical inclusivity of Jesus,' the young people said.

To mark that they themselves too would accept the invitation to the Great Feast, folk took and shared some party food from bowls set out on the table – crisps and M&Ms. 'The Kingdom of God is for all: it is life that is lived fully – filled with hope and joy. We can change the world by seeing it through the eyes of the poor, persecuted and forgotten,' the young people said.

People of all ages streamed to the table in the crossing, with names on their invitations like Asylum seekers; Those in Alcoholics Anonymous; Child abusers; Homeless people; Roma people; People who try to make a difference; Tory Party fundamentalists and the unemployed; Those who lack social skills; Aggressors, bullies, persecutors and oppressors; Drug dealers ...

The young people from Bellahouston were expressing the generosity, forgiveness and all-inclusive love of God and Jesus Christ.

To me that is amazing – and inspiring: young people are one of the most excluded groups in the world today. If I were a young person in the UK, I might have nothing but contempt and anger to serve up to an older generation who has shut them out of employment and affordable education, and wants to feed them on scraps of austerity for the next decades, after pigging out themselves for the last 50 years. On great glups of gasoline and the flesh, blood and bones of Mother Earth. I wouldn't possess that maturity; that vision and all-embracing love.

Excluding young people brings us great poverty and, as the UK 'riots' of 2011 revealed, great peril …

God, help us to make your world as all-inclusive,
as rainbow-coloured,
as Kingdom-sweet,
as a family pack of M&Ms.
Jesus Christ – ready-salt us.

Neil Paynter, from Coracle

Times when the door bursts open: the GalGael Trust visit Iona

The GalGael Trust in Govan was founded 20 years ago. It grew out of the M77 'Pollok Free State' motorway protest, when the late Colin Macleod said, 'We've shown them what we're against, now let's show them what we're for.'

Right from the outset Iona was an inspiration. During the protest, Colin and his wife, Gehan (who leads the GalGael), spent a weekend on Iona, soaking in the ancient stones and history of the place. If you walk round the GalGael workshop, you'll see many of our people carving Celtic knotwork – the symbol of eternity and interconnection – as well as some fine Celtic crosses. Also, there is a strong appreciation of nature in the totem wolves, eagles, salmon and other creatures that are a frequent feature of GalGael art.

There is also pride that George MacLeod, who was substantially responsible for rebuilding Iona Abbey, had his church in Govan. We have his secretary's old desk on our premises. It is not uncommon to hear people repeating phrases like 'Work is worship' or, as a current GalGael banner has it carved in wood, 'Work is the therapy.'

Many of our people were referred to or found out about GalGael as a part of wrestling with multiple issues such as addictions, mental health, trouble with the police, homelessness and long-term unemployment. The factor that connects all these is poverty. Through its training programme 'Journey On', GalGael uses boats and boat-building and sailing as a metaphor for life's wider journey, the pilgrimage of life.

Because of benefit restrictions and requirements, it is difficult for some of our people to leave Govan for long, so we plan most of our trips at week-ends. John Maclean, the owner of the Iona Hostel, was keen to have his place benefit us during the off-peak winter season, and for two years running now has given us exclusive use of the hostel at a most generous rate for which it was within our means to fundraise.

This year (2017) we had 28 people on the trip, all of them GalGael volunteers, 'Journey On' participants or staff/Board.

We travelled up to Iona by two minibuses and two ferry trips. Blair again volunteered to be our cook, with his partner, Illy; and as they wanted to hold a hand-fasting while on Iona, we put them in the Shepherd's Bothy as a working honeymoon.

While the GalGael is not a religious organisation, and is made up of people of many faiths and none, I had organised and sought sponsorship for this trip because we realise that, for many of our people, the spiritual journey is a vital part of their coming into a better relationship with life. This goes not just for folk who have a presenting symptom such as an addiction; it is true for all of us. Religion is important to some of our people, but most find it difficult to approach or unhelpful. There is, however, an openness to spirituality, but what does spirituality mean? The purpose of the Iona trip was to explore that question. We did so in a very open way, always mindful of Thomas Merton's emphasis on the importance of protecting '*the sanctuary of another's subjectivity*'.

After dinner on the Saturday evening I introduced the theme of spirituality. I was in the middle of suggesting that many of the problems in the world, and within ourselves, derive from an inner emptiness – when the outside door burst open. Standing there, with beaming smiles, were John, the hostel owner, and his partner, Rachael. 'We just dropped in to tell you,' he said, 'that we're so pleased to have you here on Iona.'

They left as quickly as they'd come, but their visit magically set the stage for what followed. Yes, the inner emptiness that so many of our people know is devastating, but there can be times in life when the door bursts open. Fresh avenues of welcome open up. People then divided up into groups of two or three and shared about times when they might have experienced such openings of the door in life.

After half an hour, we all got back around the table. Those who felt comfortable to do so shared from their experience. It was a very powerful session. One or two people found it a little too intense, but that is not necessarily a bad thing. Themes that emerged, both in this session and later in the weekend, included:

– *Coming to GalGael was the door that opened in my life*

– *The clear air and water of Iona*

– *Seeing people helping each other without anyone asking*

– *The GalGael faeries at play, catching things that need to be done*

– *I was frightened to give a hand, and too proud to ask for help. But now …*

– *I was against Christianity and avoided it, but I've now seen other ways of understanding it*

– *The opposite of love is not hate. You can still enjoy yourself while hating. The opposite of love is fear*

– *I'm not yet ready to speak about what weighs me down*

– *My burden has been lifted*

On the Saturday, we all went down to the Abbey to look around and see the stones in the museum. Historic Environment Scotland had provided us with free educational passes. In the Oran Chapel, Gehan sang powerfully in Gaelic from the Céile Dé tradition. On the Saturday afternoon some of us walked down to St Columba's Bay. That evening, Alan Torrance presided over a hand-fasting on the beach where Blair and Illy made commitments to each other. As the sun set in the west, the full moon rose in the east and a skein of wild geese flew overhead. As one of our people later said, 'The presences were out in force – the sunset, the moon, the geese … and it was dry.'

On the Sunday we climbed Dun I, and Linda, who is both blind and deaf, insisted on giving it a go. She made it to the top with surprising ease, thanks to Richard, her carer, and to others who gathered round her for safety.

We made it back to Govan late on Sunday evening. Since then, a number of people have commented to me how the experience was uplifting not just for them as individuals, but also for the atmosphere in our workshop as a whole. That's why this kind of experience matters. We are hugely grateful to our anonymous sponsors, and if anybody reading this would like to help us make another such visit, I'd be grateful to hear from them.

Alastair McIntosh, a founding director of the GalGael Trust (www.galgael.org) and an associate of the Iona Community, from e-Coracle

Day 24

'We can see a future together, too'

They caught me as I came into the MacLeod Centre after our morning staff meeting. One had a bucket in hand, the other pulled off her rubber gloves, having just finished morning chores. 'Could we see you today? For an hour? Even half an hour?'

We agreed to meet just before lunch. I puzzled about this young couple over the morning. What made them so keen to talk?

They were prompt. And eager. 'We'd like to have a little service this week to reaffirm our wedding vows,' he began. 'Would you help us plan it?' she went on. 'We don't know where to start.'

I had to catch my breath and think of what to say. 'Tell me about yourselves,' I said. 'Is there a special reason for a service this week?'

The couple exchanged glances. She nodded at him. He began to tell their story. They'd been through a difficult patch. Pressure at work. Very young children demanding high energy at home. They'd drifted apart. An act of betrayal had led to separation.

She took up the story. 'We came here to decide whether or not we could go on together. And it's just amazing, what's happened. We want to stay together. We know now we can.'

He continued, 'It's not just one thing that happened. But talking to other people, you know they can see a future, no matter what they've been through. And we can see a future together, too.'

That afternoon they planned the service, using prayer books and the language of love rekindling within them. It was my great honour to bless those vows in God's name. It was my delight to receive a picture from their family vacation a few months later.

Nancy Cocks, a former Director of the MacLeod Centre, from Invisible We See You

An affirmation from Iona Youth Festival

The theme of Iona Youth Festival 2015 was 'Welcome Home'. Participants – besides having a brilliant time on the pilgrimage and on a boat trip to Staffa to see the puffins – did work on the topic of immigrants and refugees/having a home and welcoming safe place to go to. At one point in the week they organised a peaceful protest around Iona, singing and carrying banners with messages such as 'Make A Change' and 'No One Is Illegal'. Following Youth Festival, the young folk took part in the 'Glasgow Sees Syria' vigil. This affirmation was read out in the Abbey during evening worship, which the young people led (Ed.).

Because God has shared his life with us, we believe that our lives are also made for sharing, and so we will always look for ways to share our time, energy and possessions with others.

Because the Kingdom of God is a safe and welcoming place, we believe that everybody, regardless of gender, sexuality or race, deserves to have a home which is their safe place. And we will do our best to make this happen.

Because the voice of God is beautiful and creative, we believe it is wrong to use words that are harmful to others, and so we will always use words that are kind and positive to build people up.

Because God has created a world of plenty, we believe that no one should be denied access to basic resources and that everyone has the right to ask for help when they need it: we will always be ready to help those who don't have what they need to flourish and will speak out on their behalf.

Because God loves and values everyone, we believe that nobody should be made to feel worthless and that everyone should feel at home in their own skin regardless of the shape or size of their own bodies. We will resist the pressure to conform to idealised 'norms' and accept and affirm each other as beautiful people.

Because Jesus confronted injustice, we believe that everyone has the right to raise their voice and take action whenever things need to be challenged and changed. So we commit ourselves to joining our voices and to helping and supporting each other in speaking out against what is wrong and in building a world which reflects the love, justice and joy of God's Kingdom.

Written by a group of 14-18-year-olds at Iona Youth Festival 2015

Day 26

In small but significant ways

In 1998, Gorbals Parish Church and Blessed John Duns Scotus Catholic Church took the significant step of signing a joint covenant. Under the terms agreed, both congregations committed themselves to action together in the local community, as a sign of their shared baptism and common discipleship.

Almost immediately, they initiated the community organisation 'Bridging the Gap'. Its aim was, and still is, to seek to bridge some of the divides that exist in this Glasgow inner-city area.

To begin with, the work was with children in the divided school system: teaching them common songs, doing shared drama, putting on joint shows, and thereby, of course, involving parents and grandparents as well.

The work in the schools greatly expanded – with workers running citizenship classes and peer tutoring across two primary and two secondary schools.

In recent years, trips have been made both to Iona and to the Corrymeela Community in Northern Ireland; horizons have been broadened, and prejudices uncovered and dealt with. There are, of course, many more divides in the local community, but by working on the basis of what can be done, rather than what can't, the work goes ahead in small but significant ways.

In these ways, the two congregations recognise and support the original aim of the covenant, hoping and praying that they can continue to witness to the Gospel together in this part of Glasgow.

John Harvey, a member of the Iona Community

Day 27

'I would have almost certainly guaranteed come out of jail in a box'

Chris Chamberlain, a volunteer with Jacob Scotland, a project for ex-young-offenders, speaks about his journey to Iona (from a press conference promoting the Jacob Project):

Right, I'll start from the very beginning …

Five years ago now I was in Reading Young Offenders … and didn't have a lot to go out to. At the time, I would class my mental health as being quite poor: I made several suicide attempts while I was in, just due to the fact that I didn't have anything whatsoever to go out to when I got released. There was nothing.

And I would be lying on my bed, in my cell, moaning about the world to my cell-mate. And I got a knock at the door. And it was the Resettlement

Officer. And I remember him going: 'You haven't got anywhere to go when you get out, have you?!' And I said: 'No.' He said: 'All right. OK,' and went away. And that was it. And I was like: *All right. Thank you very much …*

But then it was a couple weeks later, that this woman from a project called Time for God, a woman called Leslie, came to visit me in the jail. And she sat down with me in the chapel, and she said: 'If there is one thing you want to do, what would you want to do?' … I said, 'Well, I've always wanted to do youth work. But, obviously, you know, that's not gonna happen now, is it? I'm in prison.' And she said, 'No, no, bear with me, bear with me.' Then she saw someone else. And went away.

About three weeks later, she came back and said: 'Chris! Have you ever been to Scotland?'

I'm like: 'Ahhh … no.'

'How does a small island off the west coast sound?'

I went: 'Is there a pub?'

She said: 'Yes.'

'Then I'll go,' I said …

And then a few weeks after that, Helen from the Jacob Project, and Andrew, one of the staff on Iona, they came to meet me. I always remember when I was on my way down the wing to visit them, the Resettlement Officer said: 'Right – no bullshit, all right? They can tell – they can smell it a mile off.' So I'm there going: *Oh no, I wonder what's gonna happen now.* So I walked in, and I had quite a long chat, with Helen, with Andrew, about the island and such. Anyway, I got released (Jacob was working on my release). And once my tag came off, 'cause I got released on tag, I flew up to Glasgow … And if you haven't been to Iona – it's bloomin' miles away! And I got the ferry, got the bus. I always remember saying to Leslie – we were on the small ferry going across to the island – I looked out and I said: 'Look, if I see Christopher Lee or a wicker man – I'm outta here!'

And then, when I got off the ferry, the only people I saw were people with long hair and beards and sandals. So I'm like: *Oh, what have I got myself into?* So then, I got taken to the Abbey. And anyone who's been there knows that at your first meal you have to stand up and introduce yourself. And I'm like: *What do I say?: 'Hi, I'm Chris, the ex-con', or whatever?* But the welcome that I got. The warm feeling.

Afterwards, everyone just came up to me and hugged me and said: 'It's really good you're here. I'm really pleased to meet you.'

And I spent six months there, working as a housekeeper. Folding bed sheets and stuff like that. And it enabled me – well, obviously it was so far away from my hometown, I had no connection to any of my old friends, or any of my old things – there was no Internet, no mobile phones, it was complete cut-off from everything – so I was able just to take a step back and just completely rewire my brain and just start concentrating on what I actually wanted to happen.

And then, I left the island. I came here, to the Iona Community's Glasgow office, where I was working with Helen and the rest of the Youth Team as a trainee Youth Worker. Part of that role was, I started going into schools and doing a talk on my time in prison, under the title of 'Choices'.

And I always remember best, I went to this school. And then I think it was three years later, or something like that, I was working part-time on the door at a pub, and I remember a kid walked past me as I stood there and went: 'Ah! You're that dude that was in jail! You came to our school and talked.' And I was like: 'Ah, right. How you doing?' And there's this kid, he was about fourteen then, and he said: 'You know, I was very similar, on the same path as you were going. But after you came, I went home and talked to my mum and I said: "Mum, I need some help. Because I don't know what's going on. I'm hanging around with these people, doing these kinda things."'

You know, it was kind of heartwarming to see that my mistakes somehow managed to help someone else …

I'm not being melodramatic, but without the Jacob Project I would have almost certainly guaranteed come out of jail in a box … No one gives a monkey's about you when you come outta jail. No one does. My last job working in prisons, you could see it time and time and time again. It's like a revolving door, these guys are in and out, in and out. And you say 'Why?' … 'No one gives a crap about me: why should I give a crap about anything else?' Whereas the Jacob Project actually says: 'We do. We want you to fulfil your potential.'

Chris Chamberlain, a former Iona Community Youth worker and volunteer on Iona

Day 28

Prayers of concern from Iona

God who gathers us in and sends us out,
welcoming and challenging God …
We pray for all who gather in your name today:
in the centres on this island,
where worship is offered in different traditions,
which will welcome
thousands of visitors in the weeks to come –
may we find inspiration and grace for the task.

We pray for all who travel to new places,
as tourists, as pilgrims, as exiles, as refugees,

as migrants, seeking a better life –
may restless people find their rest in you.

We pray for those who come to this island
weary, and needing refreshment,
and those who come full of hope and with gifts to share –
may all know that they are needed and accepted;
may this continue to be a place of creativity and blessing.

And we pray for those who find life hard here
on this small island, with work and housing hard to find,
who are anxious for those they love,
tired, taxed in strength, troubled in mind –
give them your energy, to begin again, or to carry on.

We pray for all who gather in your name today
in places far away from here: in small rooms
as well as ancient abbeys, in drop-ins
and thrift shops, in hospital wards and works canteens,
in old people's homes, in prison chapels,
round kitchen tables, in the here and now –
may they find companionship,
share bread for the journey,
be encouraged to travel on.

We pray for the peoples of the world,
of which we are a part, a world of suffering and hope;
for places of conflict, and places of encounter;
for those who gather in solidarity, who work for peace and justice,
and those who go out to share, and to live, the Good News –
in Jesus' name

Jan Sutch Pickard, a former Iona Abbey Warden, from Gathered and Scattered

Day 29

Prayer

Iona is a very thin place.
Glasgow is something else,
or is it?

God of beauty and wonder,
of prayer and politics,
we pray for all whose lives
have been blessed and turned around by you,
whether on the island of Iona
or on country roads or city streets.
Circle them with your grace and love.
Lead them into justice and wholeness.
Bless them always
and keep them close to you.

We pray in Jesus' name
and in the Spirit's joy and power.
Amen

Ruth Burgess, a member of the Iona Community, from In the Gift of This New Day

Day 30

Iona dawn

I am by the shore
in the early darkness
when the rising sun

touches a broken world,
makes a flame
of each blade of grass,
warms the silent stones,
sends larks up
into the clean air.
The new day miracle
and the end of waiting:
I am emptied wholly
into a moment of trust
with no desire to make sense
of all this light.

Joy Mead, a member of the Iona Community, from This Is the Day

Day 31

'Everyone is welcome ...'

Something about the place called me. The excuse, almost 40 years ago now, was to take a couple of friends from France who wanted to see the Isles. But really, underneath, it was a response to some inner prompting. Waiting for the boat to take us back to the day-tripping *George V* steamer, I looked at the Abbey and heard myself say, 'I will be back here.' And for all the years after I've followed that promise, sometimes several times a year. As I stepped into a spiritual search in my late 30s, I found myself following T.S. Eliot's maxim that sometimes we return to where we started only *'to know the place for the first time'*. Youthful abandonment took me out of Christianity to lick the wounds of exclusion and judgement it had given me. But sometimes we do have to go back, in some sense, to where we started, to heal and be renewed.

On my early visits to Iona I hovered around the edges of the Iona Community and its work, entering the Abbey through its ever-open door to sit in silent contemplation, but only when no one else was there, late at night or in the early morning. Back then I was swimming the length and breadth of the New Age river – anything but the faith into which I was birthed.

But one year, on a Sunday morning, communion was about to happen, and for some reason I cannot explain to this day, I decided to go along. I sat at the back, on my own, aware that I had arrived armed to the teeth – with my guardedness, resentment, cynicism – waiting for what would surely come: some dogmatic statement about sin or damnation or Hell, or some other such unloving and excluding words. No doubt I would, as before when attending a service (the compulsory birth, marriage or death rites of passage), remain aloof to the whole show. But I was wrong-footed. No harsh words came. Instead I heard only words that were loving, questioning, tentative, humble and inclusive … I remember being overcome by a profound sense of sadness and struggled to see where this might be coming from. I was hearing words from the then Abbey Warden, Kathy Galloway, from her sermon, which were entirely welcoming and compassionate. My defences were collapsing, or being sabotaged, before my eyes.

At that moment I had the strongest sense that my parents, long-dead, were sitting either side of me. I could smell the tobacco haze that had always hovered around my dad, the scent of the Imperial Leather soap my mother loved. Communion was underway, and the Abbey suddenly seemed silent and still, even though people were moving and speaking. In this silence I heard a voice. It was a voice I had heard many times before, not so much words, more a feeling, a knowing. It said: '*You are welcome at my table. Everyone is welcome at my table. Come, eat and drink with me.*' I was struggling to hold back the tears. Three times I heard it. Then the moment passed, and I took communion.

Psychologists and sceptics could have a field day with such an experience. Maybe my inner voice was just a delusion, or an echo of the liturgy. The words – not 'come *only* if you've been baptised', or 'come *only* if you are Christian'. No: '*Everyone is welcome…*'

The power of welcome, the power of inclusion, the power of hospitality changes lives. It changed mine.

Stephen Wright, a member of the Iona Community

Month

Two

Day 1

What a witness!

One morning in October, I was asked to go down to the common room, where an unexpected visitor had arrived. On entering the room, I saw a tall robed figure standing looking out of the window. She turned when she heard me coming in, and announced, in a cut-glass English accent: 'Mr Harvey, I feel as if I have conquered Everest!'

Mother Mary, as we soon discovered, had a most impressive CV of conquering! As a young girl in the early years of the century – she was the daughter of a British Royal Navy Admiral with a Scottish aristocratic lineage – she had travelled on her own to France to help look after the many Russian refugees fleeing from the Communist takeover of their country. There, she became a member of the Russian Orthodox Church, stayed on in France, and eventually joined a Russian Orthodox religious order there, spending the rest of her life in a convent, mainly working as a translator. Now, in her latter years, she had received permission to travel back to Scotland, where, as she put it, 'I can hear again the old Scots stories and sing some of the old Scots songs before I die!' She had been given enough money from her Order to get her as far as England, where she had contacted a brother who was now a retired General, and he had funded her travel on up to Iona.

Mother Mary only stayed with us for three days. During that time, she entered with great enthusiasm into the life of the Resident group.

At the end of her short stay, I walked with her down to the jetty. On the way, she turned to me and said: 'You know, Mr Harvey, I have manic depression' (we would now say bipolar disorder) 'and I have to spend almost half of every year in hospital. I am suicidal much of the time – but I never do it, of course – my faith doesn't allow it.'

I never heard of her again – but you don't forget people like that. What a witness!

John Harvey, a former Iona Abbey Warden

Day 2

What 'penance' is about

During my time on Iona, I gained a more vital sense of what 'penance' is about. I remember one winter on Iona, welcoming a woman who had walked the forty miles across Mull in rain and wind. In the days that followed she revealed that she was doing this in order to work through an abortion she had had many years before. The walk was something she felt she 'had to do'; and I believe she went on her way with a greater sense of peace and acceptance.

Similarly, I remember one Good Friday, when it was our custom to walk the Way of the Cross through the village up to the Abbey. It fell to me that year to ask random members of the public if they would like to carry the large wooden cross for the next section. As I scanned the crowd as we gathered for prayer at a station of reflection down by the jetty, my eye picked out a tallish man, who seemed to be on his own. I gently touched his shoulder and asked him if he would like to carry the cross to the next section. He turned and fixed me with his eyes: 'I think that is what I've come for.'

I shiver goes down my spine every time I remember. We didn't speak again, but I am convinced that he went on his way healed, in the power of the Lord Jesus, but as experienced through the practice of penance.

Richard Sharples, a former Iona Abbey Warden

Day 3

Jimmy

Jimmy (not his real name) is someone I sometimes think of when I read or preach on the encounter of Jesus with the tragic man who lived in the tombs who was, as the gospel writers understood it in their time, 'tormented by devils', self-harming, throwing off his clothes and wandering through public places while his mind was confused.

After spells in psychiatric hospitals Jimmy was now in the community, but very vulnerable. He wanted to join a group spending three nights at the Abbey, because he had always wanted to go to Iona.

At the preparation meeting Jimmy had been very concerned about whether he would be able to cope and whether he would be accepted at the Abbey. He freaked out a bit over the chores, but in a very short time made breakthroughs with folk from a variety of backgrounds.

Jimmy played the guitar and sang songs he had composed. We persuaded him to do a turn at the weekly guest concert at the Mac. Jimmy gave of himself totally to this, and the clapping and cheering would have done justice to a concert-hall maestro. It reduced Jimmy to tears – of joy. This shy and awkward young man, whose confidence had so often been totally sapped, got up at the farewell meal at the Abbey. He spoke of his anxiety about coming to Iona, but of the extraordinary friendship, acceptance and support he had experienced in these last three days. He would remember this, and remember those he had befriended and lived with, as an inspiration and encouragement to him. There wasn't a dry eye in the Mac common room.

Iain Whyte, a member of the Iona Community

Day 4

Healing service, Iona Abbey

Although the month is June there is no great warmth
in here. Even our numbers don't help, and we are
about a hundred. The thick grey slate of the floor is chill.
The stone walls will not give way. There is a cool breeze
from the door that puckers the skin of my hands.
Now the minister lifts her arms and calls us into community.

I have chosen to be part of this, dipping my head in prayer.
Forcibly drawing my faith away from its natural home
into the supernatural. How far can I commit?
Cancer, anorexia, infertility, she names these things.
None of us has yet accepted the unacceptable.
One by one we go forward for the laying on of hands.

The unbearable has forced its way through our bliss.
This life is all we can be sure of. We want to go on.
Heaven and hell are where we have always lived.
There has been much talk of miracles in this place.
Much talk of a thin veil between this world and the next.
We have a great sense of togetherness, of something shared.

Rain sweeps against the windows. Candle flames shiver
in the breeze but don't go out. Human sympathy exists.
In the course of a life we all rise from the dead many times.
I know I am not who I was, who I was, who I was.
No one walks on water. Everyone walks through fire.
Once again my time has arrived. I go forward and kneel.

Robert Davidson, from Coracle

An Iona communion prayer

In the Abbey, carved on the stone altar:
'For as often as ye eat this bread and drink this cup
ye do shew the Lord's death till he come'

You feed us with bread and wine
in memory of the sacrifice of your Son, Jesus Christ,
that we may live in the fullness of faith.
Nourishing God …

You feed us together
to go out into the world
empowered by the Holy Spirit,
speaking of your love, your peace,
your strength,
so that all may know you.
Wondrous God …

And do I have to leave Iona? …

Having been fed – yes –
so that others may be fed too.

Jane Fulford

Learning to see

One Saturday afternoon, I was walking from the Iona ferry to the MacLeod Centre where I worked, chatting with a newly arrived guest who had been to Iona many times. We walked slowly for she struggled with the inclines, resting on her cane from time to time. She also had trouble with her eyes, she told me.

'But every time I come here, I feel like I can see better. The light is different here. Maybe this time God will heal my eyes.'

Her conviction was so deep! Yet, it wasn't an easy week. The weather was foul and the sea was rough. Not a great time for walking in the light she cherished. The conversation was good, though, and the week unfolded with its rhythm of daily worship, chores, programme sessions, meals and quiet chats around the fire. We didn't have another chance to talk until the final evening, when her group reflected on what they were taking home from a week on Iona.

'New friends,' said one.

'Stones!' chuckled another.

Then she spoke quietly, into a waiting pause. 'I'm going home with a reason to go on living.'

Her eyesight hadn't improved in those few days, but deep within, this woman knew what George MacLeod meant when he prayed, '*Invisible we see you, Christ beneath us.*'

Nancy Cocks, a former Director of the MacLeod Centre, from Invisible We See You

Day 7

'It wouldn't be the same without them'

The Abbey was to have two groups in it: pupils from Govan High, and member Fred Booth's adult group from Dumbarton Presbytery and his congregation in Helensburgh. For months beforehand, Fred wound me up about the mix. Abbey Warden Ian Galloway had said we would be in Abbot's House, which would at least give us a space where we wouldn't disturb the others too much.

When we arrived we were instead strung out along the East Range – with a Charismatic chiropodist and his wife at one end, and an 84-year-old couple at the other. Both groups wanted to go home, but at that time there were fortunately no boats on Sunday!

It turned out that it was the first time that the young folk were with adults who had no responsibility for them, and the adults were with young folk who they were not looking after. Both groups really got to know each other as individuals and the week produced some amazing moments. The prayers led by the young folk at the Friday night communion were among the most heartfelt I have ever heard. When Fred's group had their reunion, they insisted I brought the Govan High pupils along because *'it wouldn't be the same without them'*. For years, individuals from both groups kept in touch.

Jean Young, a member of the Iona Community and long-time Youth worker, from Coracle

Day 8

God's peace

So often Iona is perceived as a place of peace and tranquility. And of course, despite the frequent crowds of visitors between the jetty and the Abbey, many of us do discover this kind of peace here.

I had a strong sense of it the other evening walking back home towards the machair on a clear still night; in the half-darkness I could just see a tiny frog jumping across the path to keep out of my way; the croak of a corncrake penetrated the silence. And the next morning it was dry, calm and warm for the first time in a week as I went for my daily jog across the machair to Port Ban. It was so peaceful, until I encroached on the territory of the oyster-catchers at the far end of the Bay at the Back of the Ocean – they shrieked at me angrily, perhaps protecting a nest, and I thought for a moment they were going to dive-bomb me rather like terns do. In one sense it was anything but peaceful; in another sense there was harmony, mutual respect, a balance of right relationships. Real peace, deep peace does have a disturbing cutting edge; it is not just a frothy, feel-good, be-nice-to-everybody business.

When in our Iona service, we say, 'We will seek peace and pursue it,' we also say, 'We will not offer to God offerings that cost us nothing.' The peace that many people find here turns out to be very different from what they expected – not the rather sanitised 'God is in his heaven, all's right with the world' variety; more challenging and engaged than that. Along with the conviction that 'all shall be well, and all manner of thing shall be well' there is a surprising restlessness, a desire to move and change, the realisation that in our pursuit of God's peace it is our vocation to play a part in the process of resistance to all in today's culture and society that obstructs the fulfilment of God's purpose and the coming of the Kingdom.

Norman Shanks, a former Leader of the Iona Community, from a sermon in Iona Abbey

Day 9

From Uganda to Iona – a life-changing experience

Iona has been a life-changing experience for me – a chance conversation in the Abbey opened up a whole new world.

I was visiting the island with my adopted parents, Annie and Danny, when we overheard a member of staff talking about the upcoming visit of a Swedish confirmation group. So I later returned to Iona as a guest too, and then discovered that volunteers from all over the world come to help run the Centres.

Within two years I was volunteering at the MacLeod Centre – and had a great experience; then applied, and came back as a Resident at the start of the next season.

Coming from a tiny village in Uganda, it was beyond my wildest dreams that I would ever be working on Iona, meeting guests and staff from all over. Every day is a learning day for me, and I appreciate the qualities of the people I meet. I have learnt many new skills during my time here that I will use back in Uganda; and it has enabled me to save up and contribute some money to pay cousins' school fees and to support my family.

Also, with the generous support of friends, guests, well-wishers, islanders, staff and members of the Iona Community, we have all managed to raise enough money to build accessible toilets for special needs children in Uganda in two schools – a project that is still continuing: *www.gofundme.com/accessloosuganda*

I would like to thank the Iona Community for employing me and for being so generous and donating to the project in Uganda. I am looking forward to marrying my boyfriend Tom when I return to Uganda, and will use the skills I have learnt on Iona to get a job and to improve the lives of disabled children there.

I hope the Iona Community is able to offer similar opportunities to other volunteers for many years to come.

Dora Nyamwija, a former Resident group member and volunteer

Day 10

Transfiguration: a moment in Iona Abbey

Candles flicker.
Silence grows.
We wait
for God to move.
The oboe
sets its haunting melody free,
wandering,
seeking,
aching
in our souls.
Its beauty
caresses,
embraces,
holds me
in that holy,
healing moment.

Let us build them booths,
these musicians,
magicians,

muses of the Holy Spirit.
I insist!
Let us keep them
here
with us
and hold this moment,
this beauty,
to replay it
again,
again,
again.

Forever
and ever!

Then I know.
I smile
at my presumption.
The presumption of disciples
caught up in mountaintop wonder,
shrouded in beauty.
Let us build them booths, Jesus,
so that they will never leave us.

Transfiguration.
We have what has been given –
wandering,
seeking,
aching
beauty
that holds us;
heals us;
embraces us with hope.

We cannot coax
such holy wonder
to remain.
We can only live,
changed by its gift,
changed by its moment.
We can live
trusting that a gift has been given.
The gift will come again.

Nancy Cocks, a former Director of the MacLeod Centre, from Invisible We See You

Day 11

Pilgrims

The priest who travelled from Mount Athos.

The man who came from Alaska.

The man I met in the pub one afternoon, who told me he'd been camping alone on Mull, and had never felt such peace.

He worked for a big company, he said, and travelled all over the world – Hong Kong, New York, Singapore. 'Know where I was this time last week?' he asked me. 'A strip club in L.A … Know where I was the week before? … Shakespeare in London.' He ordered me a whisky with a nod people noticed, and I went over and joined him.

He sat silent a moment, then began telling me about a woman in his office who had killed herself. She sat a couple desks away; it was busy, but they talked sometimes. No one knew why she did it, they just came in one day and she was gone.

'She was beautiful. Could have had any man she wanted,' he said, and took a drink.

He went camping to get away – bought a tent, one of those camping stoves – to stop, get grounded again. When she killed herself he suddenly became aware of something down inside himself, dying too.

'I just kept seeing her empty desk every place. Know what I mean?' he asked. I nodded.

He gazed out the window; the late afternoon light glowed on the Ross of Mull, on red granite walls and columns; felt like a warm touch – on our hands, on our faces. He closed his eyes and told me that he wanted to come back here and stay longer: he had some questions.

'I went into the Abbey church – I'm not religious or anything. But felt something. I said a prayer. Lit a candle.'

Meanwhile, he'd take it around with him, he said: the peace he found, the moment he spent. 'Like a still centre. Glowing down inside yourself. Know what I mean?' he asked. I nodded.

We spoke a little longer; he was dying to tell someone he said. He ordered me another malt whisky; then got up and went out on the small talk left. I could see him out the window. Standing, gazing out at the sea.

I thought about all he'd told me, and about how much of my time I spend flying around, or sitting closed up in a corner.

Like God was telling me that if I just stopped, just glanced up from me a moment, there was a world of deep experience and communion waiting. People behind newspapers and office desks dying to talk, sunsets ripe as fruit. Life in all its fullness.

I became aware of the choice of every moment: Looking up, or looking down. Reaching out, or folding in. Flying away, or standing firm. Feeling, or unfeeling.

Living or dying.

Neil Paynter, from Iona: Images and Reflections

Day 12

'Thus shall these walls be justified' (Urban Priority Areas Week on Iona)

Oban pier, 1:50pm, Saturday 14th July, 2012. Two bus-loads of excited people spill out onto the tarmac, heading for the ferry to Mull – that's due to leave at 2:00pm! The word goes out: 'Don't take time to look for your own bags – just grab what you can carry and *run*!' And we all got on – with all the luggage. What an exercise in trust – and what a great start to a holiday!

In summer 2012, the Church of Scotland Priority Areas team, led by Martin Johnstone and Lynn MacLellan, took a group of 35 adults and 46 children to the Iona Community's three centres – the Abbey, the MacLeod Centre and Camas – for a week. The families came from ten Urban Priority Area parishes in Glasgow and three nearby towns.

What were the highlights? The weather – stunning for the first three days, *dreich* and then soaking for the middle two – then stunning again for the last two. The islands of course – most folk managed to get to at least one beach, some more than once. The Centres – people loved the Abbey, and took over the Mac with gusto, while the teenagers revelled in all that Camas had to offer. The Community's staff – several going way beyond their allotted hours and job descriptions in offering help and support. The programme

– we had stories from Jan Sutch Pickard, 'Worship in the Wild' with Jo Love, games all over the place with Neil Young and the Community's youth staff, two boat trips with Davie Kirkpatrick (to Staffa in the afternoon, round the south end of Iona in the evening), the off-road and on-road pilgrimages (the latter just made it to Martyrs' Bay for lunch, quite an achievement considering the various stop-offs for chips on the way), arts and crafts in the Mac, abseiling and kayaking at Camas, two ceilidhs, breadmaking, music-making, pizza-making, candle-making, bedtime stories for the wee ones, an indoor barbecue, a closing concert. And we even had our very own 2012 Olympic Games. The games were held in the village hall, due to the weather, and ended with a race through the grounds of the Nunnery. We even had our own medal ceremony!

Did the families enjoy themselves? One granny, with tears in her eyes, confessed that 'no one has ever given me a holiday before'. People spoke of the unique experience of getting away together as a family; of the pleasure of getting food put down in front of them; of the programme for the children, which gave them 'time off'; of the way everyone looked out for each other; of the beauty of the island and of the story of the Abbey. A mother shared her surprise at how religion on Iona was about 'the ordinary things – I expected it to be all holy!'; another called the whole experience 'humbling – a total privilege'. A single mum, who had been initially quite cautious about the holiday, shared how she gradually felt more and more comfortable, and 'I love the way you say the Psalms in the services'. 'It was magic!' someone else said of the time. An asylum seeker said that it was brilliant to get the opportunity to come here: 'When you are locked in Glasgow, you don't realise how beautiful places like this are.' Some had come expecting a bit more peace and quiet – most had really no idea of what to expect. One three-year-old, trying to explain how it felt on the boat trip to the south end of the island, as the swell began to rock the boat, pronounced 'the boat's gone kind of curly'! Tears and laughter were shared.

So yes – the families enjoyed the holiday. For some, especially mothers with young or particularly challenging children, there were times of struggle; one such mum, offered a wee while off while her children were in the crèche, announced gratefully: 'I'm just going to enjoy a shower to myself.' Older children often acted as 'au pairs' for some of the mums with younger children, which was a tremendous help. The end refectory table in the Abbey was set up with Lego for the wee children at mealtimes. As for the staff team, it's probably true to say that everyone felt it was a tremendously worthwhile week, and a privilege to be involved and to meet and get to know so many courageous and amazing people.

Tricia McConalogue, from Bridging the Gap, wrote: 'The staff at the Mac were brilliant at initiating conversation at the dinner table and getting to know the families. They also knew the children by name. Their patience with the children was great too, allowing them to ring the bell for mealtimes. The Mac was lively and vibrant and the staff seemed to welcome this buzz. One evening the people who were helping to wash the dishes in the kitchen started a sing-song. The staff joined in and afterwards one of the staff thanked the women, saying this really made her day ... For me it had the attributes of Braendam House, that being there for each other, looking out for each other, noticing if someone wasn't at the table and going to look for them, just what Jesus would do. It would be great if Iona was made available for more families like this.'

In conclusion, we'd like to think that George MacLeod, once he'd got over the sight and sound of all these children in the Abbey, was smiling down on it all, and saying softly to himself, in the words of one of his famous prayers: '*Thus shall these walls continue to be justified.*'

John and Molly Harvey, members of the Iona Community, from Coracle

Day 13

Iona morning

A painterly prospect.
Light on things:
the way the rising sun
touches smallness: a fusion
of flowers, unidentified;
the wood of the compost bin
looking as if a moment ago
someone left in a hurry
leaving a task unfinished.

Far off against the sea the ruins of a room,
nearer the beginning or end of a wall.
There will always be fragmentary walls

as we might think there will always be
the Abbey. The same light touches
all and I stand waiting in the cool dew
of a morning that is now, for always
and could be the beginning of time.

Joy Mead, a member of the Iona Community, from A Way of Knowing

Day 14

'That's the way we like it back home'

We had finally convinced our people to get on the train in North Wales, early in the morning, and after a peaceful evening in Oban, they were lapping up the Iona experience. We were sharing the MacLeod Centre with a group of prayerful women from Eastern Europe, who compensated for their struggles with English by kindly trying to overfeed my pregnant wife. 'Must eat more. Good for baby!'

A day or two in, we had become very fond of each other.

In the Abbey was an ecumenical group from Northern Ireland, led by a Methodist minister (who had been very impressed by the singing of our group in the pub) and a Catholic priest, to whom it fell one night to give an address in a service. And so he did. At great length. About the trials of his people. I think he was doing it ad lib – he just kept thinking of more and more details. And I became concerned for the Eastern European women, who would barely be following what he said.

Over after-service tea, I noticed that they were looking very pleased. 'Did you understand what our friend was saying?' I asked. 'Oh no!' came the reply, 'but it was *long*. That's the way we like it back home!'

David Coleman, a member of the Iona Community

Day 15

From Cuba to Iona – on the same journey

It is hard to express with words how many feelings the visit to Iona made me experience. The nature and the sunset, the colours, the peacefulness. As we were walking and seeing all those ancient places and the crosses it was for me like an affirmation of my faith.

The other thing that made a large impression on me, after the history of Iona, was the ability to bring so many people from all over the world and of different faiths together. To be able to meet them and worship with them. This was a very fulfilling time for me. I met people from Germany, Australia, the USA, Scotland, from different paths and different theological backgrounds. We were on the same journey: the journey of living spirituality and action for justice and peace in the world. To be in front of the cross took me back to my calling. God called me to serve and follow him, working for the kingdom of justice, love and peace.

Joel Dopico, Pastor of the Presbyterian Reformed Church in Cuba,
after a visit to Iona in 2008, from Coracle

Day 16

We bring our unique gifts (from a service in Iona Abbey)

Ephesians 4:11–16

Leader: The Iona Community is an ecumenical Christian community. Living and working on Iona on behalf of the Iona Community is a diverse group of people. We come from many different backgrounds and Churches:

My name is Tom. I come from a Quaker background. I was brought up to be peaceful and thoughtful. For me worship is a time to reflect and find peace.

My name is Elisabeth. I come from an Episcopalian background. I was brought up to love and trust God. For me worship is an extension of my relationship with God.

My name is Junko. I come from a mixture of a Buddhist and Shinto background. I was brought up not to forget thankfulness to anything, anytime. For me worship is to express my thankfulness for everything, especially for nature. Nature is God for me.

My name is Ines. I come from an atheist background. I was brought up to mistrust religion, but found my faith in God as a young adult. For me worship is a platform to encounter God.

My name is Carole. I come from a Roman Catholic background, and the liturgies, spirituality and music of that are still important to me, though my search for God has also led me to explore more earth-based practices such as druidry. For me worship is an opportunity to reorient my inner compass towards God.

My name is Pip. I come from an Anglican background. I was brought up in a formal, traditional Church of England church, but now worship in a charismatic, non-denominational community church. For me worship is connecting with my eternal Lover, Father and Mother, rejoicing losing myself in the Creator's great Love.

Leader: In the conventions of our society, labels are always being placed on us. Sometimes we let them define us. But they don't need to. In this place, all are welcome … We are a living, breathing community of Christ. We bring our unique gifts and offer them …

From Coracle

Day 17

The story of the sower

In 2000 I brought a group of 33 people to Iona from our church community project in Sheffield. These folk were of all ages. Some stayed in the MacLeod Centre, but because so many had wanted to come some stayed in local B and Bs and self-catering places. We came together to worship at the Abbey each day and took part in the pilgrimage, some went to Staffa, and whilst we were on Iona we baptised three of our young people in the sea at Martyrs' Bay. This is still remembered as being 'just like a scene from the Bible'.

At the time we used a strategy called 'remembering the Bible' at our Sheffield project. It's an oral strategy for retelling and interpreting the gospel with people of all ages and abilities. Many of the folk from the project were new to the Bible, and telling the stories, rather than reading them, was more engaging and creative in our context. People joined in readily and made the Bible their own.

I remember walking back from the village one night with some other guests and some of our folk. I was near the back of the group but I could clearly hear, through the darkness, the voice of one of our group telling another about the remembering the Bible strategy. The guest he was speaking to was a priest from Ireland and the story he was telling him was the story of the sower: 'So, for example, the story of the sower, it goes like this … and that's about us and how God looks after us who live on the edge of the city where we haven't got much except this project to help us – but just look at how many of us are here this week!'

Listen then if you have ears.

Janet Lees

Day 18

The good shepherd (reflection from an Iona Abbey welcome service)

I live on a croft here, at the north end of Iona. Our lambing finished a few months ago, in fact they go away to market tomorrow. But back in April, as usual, we had a few lambs that needed extra help with bottle-feeding, as their mothers didn't have enough milk.

Within two days these lambs know the person who feeds them – they recognise you from a distance – and they come running. If you call to them at other times, they still run to you. Sheep and lambs on Iona are generally pretty lucky; they are well cared for.

My husband, Iain, used to have a full-time job as a stonemason here at the Abbey, but every spring, throughout lambing, he would get on his quad bike and go home during his coffee break, his lunch break and his afternoon tea break to check each sheep due to lamb, and to check each sheep that already had lambs. We bottle-feed the weaker lambs at breakfast, lunch, dinner and supper every day, sometimes more often if they are really struggling. On the way to the north end Iain would pass other crofts, and each year there would be at least half a dozen times when he would have to get off the quad and jump into somebody else's field: to put a fallen ewe back up on her feet, to deliver a stuck lamb, or to drive away crows attempting to peck out the eyes of a newborn lamb. He didn't just worry about his own flock, he had an eye for all the other animals along the road. That is why this parable struck me. Jesus says:

'I am the good shepherd. I know my own and my own know me … and I lay down my life for the sheep. I have other sheep that do not belong to this fold. I must bring them also, and they will listen to my voice. So there will be one flock, one shepherd …' (John 10:14–16, NRSV)

When Jesus told this story, he was talking to people who completely understood what was involved in shepherding. They knew what Jesus was taking on, what he was promising them. Like many of you, I grew up in a town, and until I came here, I had only the vaguest ideas about looking after animals. But when you live with a shepherd, you start to realise what is involved, and you end up understanding that Jesus is taking on absolutely every aspect of our lives, intensively, intimately: he accepts your foot rot, your maggots, your wilfulness and ignorance, as well as the times you skip along the sand dunes and lie in the sun.

It seems to me that we are being told to watch out for everyone – not just our families, our friends, the people in our own fold. There are other people out there, and we must care for them too.

Carol Dougall, from Coracle

Day 19

Dare to ask

When I was staying at the MacLeod Centre in late August one year, some of us were looking for the opportunity to have close discussions about important questions, ideas, even doubts around our faith. So, on two afternoons, I dared to invite people into a discussion group around the fire, and came up with some questions to share. One of them was 'I don't believe in hell as a place where God punishes people for being sinners after their death … do you?'

It was amazing and so reassuring how many people in the group confirmed also that 'hell' is not an actual place within their own beliefs. So many of the questions which I 'dared to ask' the group helped me to feel stronger and less alone with my own faith. It actually was my first step on an exciting pathway to explore and begin writing my new book (*What Do I Believe?*) about our modern understandings of Jesus, and of the word 'Christian'.

I now am in the process of holding meetings with people from different denominations, as well as people who do not belong to a traditional 'church' but still have very strong connections to Jesus, where I do not offer my own ideas but simply ask questions and, without judgement, listen closely and record what the person replies. It is truly inspiring, and humbling, how the people I meet offer me such a wide range of beliefs/understandings/interpretations of Jesus and the Bible, and yet at core are all so simply connected. Sometimes their answers are not what I believe at all, but at these times I often learn more, by listening to and respecting other approaches to God.

So my week on Iona set me off on a journey which is teaching me how much we can learn and give and receive when we do 'dare to ask', guided by the courage, curiosity and honesty of our loving faith.

Jacci Bulman is the author of A Whole Day Through From Waking *(Cinnamon Press, 2016).*

Day 20

Why are we here?

In the early 1970s, while Molly and I were part of the Resident group in the Abbey, we had a visit from a group of American college students, who stayed with us for two weeks in the summer. It was the height of the Vietnam War. Many of the students had been deeply engaged in protests against their government's involvement in the war. Their college chaplain was very supportive of their actions, but wanted to find a way of helping them to get in touch with the age-old Christian heritage of action for justice and peace, as many of them were alienated from the traditional churches in America, or were quite put off by the strident tones of the popular evangelistic preachers of the day.

So he conceived of a plan to bring them to Europe. He took them first to a monastic community in France – it might have been Taizé, I can't now remember the details – then to an Anglican community in the south of England, and finally to us on Iona. His idea was that the students would encounter Christian groups who were both actively engaged in action for justice and peace in their own contexts and drank deeply from the spiritual tradition of the Universal Church, and sought to express this in the whole of their lives – in their actions and in their worship, and remained connected to the church, while at the same time being comfortable with living at times on the edges of it.

We certainly had a memorable fortnight! By the time they reached us, the students were quite tired, and not too enthusiastic about getting involved in the daily life of the Abbey – chores, services, talks, etc. By the end of the first week, some of our colleagues on the Abbey staff were getting a bit disgruntled with the Americans, to put it mildly. Both the chaplain and I realised that something needed to be done. So we called a meeting – essentially, I suppose, what used to be called a greetin' meetin' – with our staff and the students, to try to clear the air. It was held in the Chapter House, where in medieval times similar greetin' meetings were held every week by the monks. Honest, and at times difficult, words were spoken, there were a few tears, and eventually the air was indeed cleared. And the second week went much better all round. I didn't hear from them after they left, so I don't know whether the chaplain's plan worked – did they get back involved with protests against the Vietnam War with a deeper understanding of the Christian roots of their action, as a result of their European tour? And were they able to reconnect in some way with the church back in America? I hope so.

But that whole experience came to mind just the other day, as I was reading the chapter on faith in Krista Tippett's amazing book *Becoming Wise: An Inquiry into the Mystery and Art of Living*. Krista Tippett hosts a public radio programme called *On Being* in America; she has interviewed hundreds of scientists, theologians, activists, film stars and scores of others – and she always manages to draw out from them their 'spirituality', not necessarily in any religious sense, but deeply personal: *'that which ultimately motivates them'*, to borrow a phrase that Kathy Galloway has used.

In her chapter on faith, she tells of the growth in America of the 'Nones': the people who write 'None' when asked to fill in their religious affiliation on census forms. And she explores the way in which some of this young 'Nones' generation, who *'are not people who affiliate themselves with any religious communities in particular'*, are *'drawn to something that is in these traditions. They recognise that something is there, and they don't feel that they can go to the existing institutions to explore them. So they're playing around on their own.'*[1]

Tippett sees a connection between this searching generation and the movement called the New Monasticism. She describes it in some detail, and sums it up thus: *'The Nones of this age are ecumenical, humanist, trans-religious. But in their midst are analogs to the original monastics: spiritual rebels and seekers on the margins of established religion, pointing tradition back to its own untamable, countercultural, service-oriented heart.'* Her view of this sort of reconnection with religious tradition is by no means rose-tinted; she goes on to recognise that it can also lead to extremism.

Nevertheless, when I read what she is talking about, I immediately see a connection with what I think we have been, and still are, about in our Centres on Iona. In the prayer for the Iona Community, part of our daily prayer, we ask that God will first of all grant to the present-day church the gifts of *'courage, faith and cheerfulness'* that God gave to Columba. Only then do we go on to ask that God will *'further in all things the purpose of our Community'*, which we define as finding '*new ways to touch the lives of all*'. Thus, in our daily prayer, we look in to the church, and then out to the whirling world around us – '*in the sweep of the drama of human history and the contemporary globe*', to use Krista Tippett's powerful phrase – and seek God's help to bring the two together, so that lives may be touched, and changed. That, it seems to me, is why we are on Iona at all – and why, by God's grace, we seek to stay there, still.

John Harvey, a member of the Iona Community, from Coracle

1. Krista Tippett quotes from *Becoming Wise: An Inquiry into the Mystery and Art of Living*, Penguin Random House, 2016

Day 21

Another day

Another day –
a day that God has made –
the sky is mother-of-pearl
like the inside of a seashell;
the sea is moving darkness
and then dancing with light
as the sun rises over Mull.
Every stone has its own shadow,
every blade of grass is shining.
Alarm clocks go off,
feet hit the floor,
porridge is on the stove,
bells ring,

feet are on the stairs,
toast smells good,
folk gather,
grace is said,
a hundred cups of tea are poured,
the sun climbs the sky
and the big bell rings for worship.
Feet are on the road.
Now the world is on the move,
wheels are turning,
ships putting out to sea,
cows coming to the milking,
shops opening,
a catch being landed,
computers being switched on,
school bells ringing.
On the far side of Mull
bus engines start up,
wheels begin to turn.
As the sun travels across the sky,
folk travel toward Iona,
to the ferry:
the day visitors, tourists, trippers,
pilgrims on their way
at the beginning of the day –
the day that God has made.

Jan Sutch Pickard, a member of the Iona Community, from Out of Iona

Day 22

By God's grace

If Iona was in the States,
some developer would have scooped it up by now,
building high-rises at Martyrs' Bay,
a casino on the machair
and transforming the Abbey into a mall of shops …

But, by God's grace, Iona still is
that thin place that casts a wide shadow across all borders,
that island where strangers become lifelong friends,

where weathered crosses babysit children and lambs,
where silence is welcomed and laughter encouraged,
where introverts discover storytelling gifts,

that tiny speck of land
which gathers people from all over the world –
and sends them out to continue
their pilgrimage back home,

that community which uses not only stone to rebuild,
but justice to establish new hope,
compassion to mend broken lives,
new music to tell the ancient story.

Thom M. Shuman, an associate of the Iona Community

Day 23

The thick places (from a sermon in Iona Abbey)

George MacLeod is often quoted as saying Iona is a thin place – with small boundaries between the material and spiritual. Only the thickness of a tissue between heaven and earth. I love this and I experience it here. This seems to me to be a place *'shot through with the Glory of God'*. It's so important to have this experience precisely because it helps us, it nurtures us, when we're in the THICK places – the God-forsaken places, the ugly places – places of death and oppression where Jesus' presence can hardly be felt or experienced with any spontaneity.

These are places where Christ comes to us in the guise of a stranger – in the hookers, crooks and thieves just like the crowd Jesus made his best friends and in whom he promises to hide himself.

Is not our spiritual pilgrimage a daily journey of taking up the cross to see the presence of God – to see the executed and risen Christ in the most unlovely places so that we can be led to resist and struggle and advocate and agitate and present our bodies as living sacrifices against all that hurts and maims and insults and kills God's children? This is not an easy pilgrimage because it inevitably brings conflict with the powerful and *'the money boys'*, as George MacLeod loved to call them. Struggling for the poor and exploited means pushing with all our strength against the powerful tides of global capitalism and its maniacal, frenetic demands to buy more, consume more, trample our neighbours, and ignore the common good in our desperate pursuit of our own personal comfort, titillation, pleasure and convenience. And this struggle is never welcomed by the powers.

Our hearts are set on pilgrim roads not to satisfy ourselves with finding one holy place, not to romanticise this thin place, but to take the experience of the presence of the Holy back into the thick of things …

Murphy Davis, the Open Door Community, USA, http://opendoorcommunity.org

Day 24

Praying under my fig tree

It is just about a year since I moved from an isolated, large house with a large garden to a one-bedroomed, ground-floor flat with a small garden. I enjoy the ease of caring for a smaller place and the closeness to shops, church and public transport, but there are a few things I miss. I especially miss the nooks and crannies in my former garden, but most of all I miss my fig tree. It is not just the abundant crop of luscious fruit that I long for. It is the 'special place' under the fig tree.

From the moment we planted the tree in 1986, it was special. We planted it in front of a ten-foot-high, south-facing wall where it would get the benefit of the sun and shelter from the cold north winds. The first thing I thought about when I stood back to admire it was the story of Nathanael (John 1). Nathanael asked Jesus, 'How do you know me?' And Jesus answered, 'I saw you under the fig tree.'

I could not go near my fig tree without thinking of that story, so it became, for me, a special place of prayer. We spend so much time in life wearing masks, playing roles and living up to other people's expectations, that I find that there is something very healing, very peaceful, very consoling, just to be able to sit and be me and know that I am completely loved and accepted by God. That is how I felt under my fig tree.

Most people will have experienced a special place that seems more conducive to prayer and where their physical and spiritual lives become more integrated. For many people, Iona is that special place, but sadly, for most of us, it is not in our back garden. I remember sitting at the north end of Iona with a friend, looking out at Staffa and the cliffs of Mull. After a long time she said, 'How could anyone sit here like this and not praise God?' Her words echoed my own thoughts.

I also remember a session when I stayed at the Abbey many years ago. We had had a wonderful week and all the guests were saying how they had found peace, a spiritual uplift and closeness to God. We were told that what we had felt, we had brought with us – within us – and that we would still have it within us when we left. If that is so, maybe I do not need my fig tree. It may be a little more difficult to find that feeling of complete peace, love and acceptance, but it is there to find.

Pat Welburn, a member of the Iona Community, from Gathered and Scattered

Day 23

The work of God

I can never come down the stairs into the north transept without thinking of our predecessors here – the Benedictine monks of the thirteenth to fifteenth centuries. I know these aren't the actual stairs they used, but near here they came down, night after night, summer and winter, into the Abbey church to say the night office. No central heating, no electric light – just doing it, doing the 'work of God', as they saw it, because that was what they had committed themselves to. When we used to feel sorry for ourselves (as I guess people still do from time to time up on Iona!) – too busy, stressed, not coping, fed up with guests or day tourists or just ourselves –

I used to think of these anonymous monks coming down that night stair, heavy with sleep, and … well, just give myself a shake. We stand in a great tradition of commitment – and the daily, nightly 'work of God', whatever it may be.

John Harvey, a former Iona Abbey Warden, from Bare Feet and Buttercups

Day 26

Postcards from Iona

You will know the place,
the sweep of the bay,
the way down to the waves,
the particularity of
each path and pebble
as it waits to be chosen.

You will know the seat
where I sit to write and wonder
what each of you will feel
when the card arrives.
Will you hear
a chorus of memories?
Will you see
your child selves:
racing across the sand,
leaping waves,
loving the freedom?
Today my hands are full
of shadows and the song
the wind sang

in the nunnery ruins
is made up of fragments
of moments – earthed
in a place so lovely
that looking hurts
almost.

This is truly an isle
full of noises – its secret
whispered across the water
and in each drop of rain
as it begins to fall
on the words I write.

Joy Mead, a member of the Iona Community, from A Way of Knowing

Day 27

Sauce bottle

'Sauce bottle' wasn't his real name of course. In fact, it wasn't even his real nickname.

His name was Robbie McGinley, and his real nickname was 'SB' – short for sauce bottle, I expect. For as long as anyone could remember, Robbie had a penchant for liberal dollops of tomato ketchup on everything he ate. There were even stories of tomato-sauce-flavoured ice cream. Whatever the truth was, Robbie McGinley and tomato sauce were a legendary combination.

Robbie never took to the nickname 'sauce bottle'. 'He goes nuts if you call him that,' I was told. So SB it was – anything to stop a young man going nuts. In fact, SB was prone to going nuts fairly regularly. That's what got him into trouble. Trouble and SB – like Robbie McGinley and tomato sauce

– were pretty well inseparable. He'd 'done time' in List D schools and YOIs (young offender institutions). It seemed it wouldn't be long before SB and the inside of an adult prison would form a lasting acquaintance.

SB found his way to Iona with some other lads from a local outreach project on his estate. He'd not really wanted to go, but his best mate, Dekko, had signed up, and, anyway, SB had nothing particular planned that week. It was in the days of the old youth camps, when youth work on Iona had its own unique style – a bit rough and ready, working at a lot of different levels, and changing lives. And one of those was SB's.

Unbeknown to most of the lads from the estate, the group gathered together in the youth camp that week was as varied as you could get – and on purpose. There were kids like SB and Dekko, already on the slippery slope to major problems; there were lads from a YOI, on a pre-release pro-gramme; there were what were known then as 'handicapped' people and their able-bodied carers; there were teenagers with learning difficulties; and there was a smattering of youth and project workers.

'Why you called SB when your name's Robbie?' one of the special-needs kids asked after the introductory session.

'If you fucking find out and tell anyone, I'll bloody pan ye, ye crippled doughnut.'

'Hey, it's no' fair. SB never takes his turn at the chores.'

'Shut yer face, Thicko, ah'm daein' nae lassie's work.'

It was going to be that sort of week.

A lot could be written about SB as the week unfolded – good and bad – and a lot will never ever be clear – because all of that was going on in SB's head. But what was obvious to everyone was that things were changing. 'Thicko' – aka Bobby – actually learned table tennis from SB, and Bobby and SB reigned supreme in the doubles tournament by the end of the week. 'Crippled doughnut' – aka Sandra – had a squad of lads lifting her wheelchair over rocks, and SB was the foreman organiser and Sandra's minder. And I swear I saw a tear in SB's eye when the week's participants were boarding the ferry for the journey home – or maybe it was just a bit of sea spray that had splashed his face.

I learned later that Bobby and Sandra had arranged for a present to be given to SB at the end of the week. Maybe it's because SB had cleaned the youth camp kitchens out of tomato ketchup by the last day – well, people notice these things, don't they? Or maybe they'd found out something SB didn't really want them to know. But I gather no panning of innocent people took place. And, rumour has it, there's a bottle of tomato sauce on the top shelf in SB's bedroom that's got pride of place, that's never been opened, and, I suspect, will never be.

Tom Gordon, a member of the Iona Community, from Gathered and Scattered

Day 28

Song for Iona

Iona of the isles
Iona of the seas
Iona of my heart

Iona of the wild geese
of the high-standing cross
of the ancient, weathered stone

Iona of the layered skies
the boggy lanes
the rainbow shower

Iona of the freezing church
the stripped altar
the howling winds

Iona of the markings
of the wounding
of the arrow of desire

Iona of Easter morning
of the deluge,
a woman running, frantic, in darkness

Iona of the resplendent church
the blazing candles
the floral cross

Iona of the music
of the meetings and friendship
of remembrance and healing

Iona of the porridge bowl
the fresh-made bread
the breakfast tables

Iona of the departing ferry
the hugs and tears of farewell
the final views across the Sound

Iona of the isles
Iona of the seas
Iona of my heart

Nicola Slee

Day 29

Breaking the chains that bind us

On my first visit to Iona, I was a guest travelling with a group of mainly young adults with learning disabilities. It was a 'mountaintop' week, with the theme of 'Breaking the chains that bind us'. One young autistic man, with no formed verbal speech and a lot of agitated energy, was the trigger for a number of revealing experiences during the week. But perhaps my most vivid memory was of the midweek guest worship during which the gathered folk were draped and entwined in long paper chains. The climax of the worship, well-crafted by an imaginative programme worker, was everyone jumping up and throwing off the chains to be led by the young man – with boundless noise and whooping – in a dance out into and around the cloisters of the Abbey. Perhaps one of the few times in his life that young man was in the lead and at the centre of everything.

Yvonne Morland, a member of the Iona Community

Day 30

A place where both our faith and commitment could be strengthened

A journey from the U.S. state of Georgia to Iona is not a simple thing. My wife Leslie and I began planning our pilgrimage more than six months in advance. The themed week starting May 26, 2012 was the perfect time to go: resource leaders Mark Braverman and Naim Ateek would lead a week of discovery on the Israeli occupation of Palestine. As long-time activists for peace and justice, we knew a fair bit about the issue, but had not been active in recent years. We were casting about for the best way to get re-involved in work for peace. We had briefly visited the island before, and knew from a pilgrimage then that Iona was a place where both our faith and our commitment to justice could be strengthened. We put in our application for the week, and found flights from Atlanta to Edinburgh. Perfect!

We needed to get in a little better physical condition before the trip. An overnight hike in the north Georgia mountains two weeks before our departure would be a good warm-up, we thought. Then disaster struck. A few hundred yards into the hike, Leslie's toe caught a tree root and she went down. Her knee hit the granite that undergirds our mountains here. Several of us improvised a stretcher from a backpack frame and carried her back to the car. Within hours she was in surgery having a badly fractured kneecap wired together.

I was pretty discouraged about the trip, but not Leslie. No sooner was she out of the hospital than a flurry of e-mails flew between us and the Community. We were assured we were still very welcome to come, and that Leslie's temporary handicap would be accommodated. With the hesitant approval of her surgeon, we were off.

The flight was not without its moments, but we made it to Edinburgh, where an airport employee wheeled Leslie through doors marked 'Staff Only' to immigration and customs officials, who gave us quick clearance. Eventually, we made it to the Abbey – with everybody along the way going out of their way to be helpful.

Leslie and the scooter quickly became part of the scene, with people rushing ahead to open doors for her. When the rest of the group went on the weekly pilgrimage around the island, Jan Sutch Pickard, the MacLeod Centre Director, led Leslie and others with mobility issues on a mini-pilgrimage around the Abbey and nearby points of interest. The programme on Israel and Palestine was highly informative and inspiring – we participated in the drafting of the 'Iona Call' and witnessed the birth of Kairos Britain (*www.kairosbritain.org.uk*).

When we came back to Georgia we quickly plunged into similar work here.

Mark Reeve, an associate of the Iona Community

Day 31

Arguing with God

In 1952/53 I was away from my home in New Zealand for two years. I spent some time in Manchester, where I met Tom Colvin, who was a member of the Iona Community. He arranged for me to be the 'odd job' man at the Argyll Hotel on Iona for the three months of summer.

The rebuilding of the Abbey was still a long way from completion. Tom introduced me to George MacLeod, and I attended many worship services. I was bowled over by George's sermons. His brand of Christianity was so down to earth and relevant to real life.

Strange feelings began to come to me while I was on Iona. These were reinforced when I was walking along the village street one day. A group of women, including my boss, Mrs Campbell, were having a heated discussion. They were upset by something. I don't know whether it was the Iona Community or the local minister. One of the ladies turned to me and said, 'When are *you* a minister?' I said: 'Oh, no! I'm not going to be a minister!'

But the feeling that I was being pushed in that direction persisted.

One day I sat down on a stile on my way to get milk from a croft on the other side of the island, and had it out with God. I said: 'There is no way I can be a minister: I was at high school for only two years. How can I go to university? The Presbyterian Church of New Zealand requires a university education before anyone can be accepted into theological college.'

That was the end of the matter, or so I thought. The very next day I stopped in the village street to talk to a young fellow I had got to know, who was a youth associate of the Community. He said, 'Why don't you go to university while you're in Scotland?'

I replied that I couldn't do that because I had been at high school for only two years! He said, 'Oh, that's no problem. There are special schools in Scotland that prepare you for entrance to university.' I was absolutely shocked. How did he know what was going on in my head? I hadn't told anyone about that. Suggesting that somebody go to university is not the sort of thing one person says to another every day. God was not leaving me alone after all.

I wrote home to my mother and asked her to make enquiries. She found out that it was even easier in New Zealand in those days: if you were over 21 you could go straight into university in what was called provisional entrance.

So my excuse was gone! Now I have been ordained for over 55 years.

Keith Weavers, an associate member of the Iona Community in Australia

Month

Three

Day 1

God's healing work

One day, word came to me of a strange couple who had arrived unannounced, and were causing a bit of a stir in the Abbey church. I went over, to discover a man kneeling in front of the Communion table, and a woman standing by the baptismal font, who announced, when she saw me, 'You will marry me to the Devil tonight.'

It turned out that this couple had been patients in a psychiatric hospital. Somehow, they had managed to leave, and had got themselves over to Iona, where they stayed for most of the rest of the week. I can't now remember where they actually slept, but they caused quite a lot of anxiety amongst our Resident group, at one point even trapping our Coffee House manager in her room while the woman tried on Anne's dresses. They were clearly in a very bad way – eventually, the woman decided to leave on her own by walking across the Sound, and was hauled out of the water by some of the islanders, and the man left by the more traditional ferry route. We were, as you can imagine, confused and relieved – confused, because we felt we hadn't really done anything to help them, and relieved, because we knew we weren't set up to offer the sort of help they had needed anyway.

But the story has a happy ending. Two years later, I was asked to go down to the cloisters to meet a couple with a baby who wanted to see me. And there they were, altogether in much better shape, and with a lovely wee girl – they had come back to thank us for what they felt had been our care for them when they had been here. They had gone back to the hospital, had eventually been discharged, and had found their way to a caring little community of people in Glasgow.

Again, I don't know what happened to them after that – all I can say is that I believe God's healing work took place, despite our misgivings, for them on Iona – and continued, through the hospital, and then through the community of people in Glasgow.

John Harvey, a former Iona Abbey Warden

Day 2

The wild wonder of Iona

I arrived on Iona on a bone-chilling day in late January. A few days later, hurricane-force winds whipped around us. The ferry across the Sound of Iona sensibly stayed in its shelter, but island life continued as normal – at least until the power went out. I ventured outside, thinking that, as a Canadian, I had seen the wind. But that wind flipped me around and tossed me against a gate without a thought. When I saw a roof slate fly past, I reconsidered my courage.

That night around nine o'clock, the wind dropped suddenly.

Again I made my way outdoors, enjoying the subtle glow from coal fires and candlelight reflected in still-darkened windows. The moon was full, its trail of light glistening on the water. The air was calm but I could hear a constant roar, as if the wind still echoed in my head. It was the voice of the sea. I stared at the water in wonderment. The sea was charged with energy. Waves galloped down the Sound, racing against each other. In the brilliant moonlight, the crest of each wave shimmered like the mane of a wild horse celebrating its freedom. Such power. Such threat. Such beauty. Such grace.

The beauty of Iona astonished me again and again. On a sunny summer day, the sea's deep turquoise laps against white sand beaches and brooding black rock formations. In winter, the sun drops in for a few blessed hours, offering fragile light that plays with shadows on surrounding cliffs from its vantage point far to the south. The sky changes with the wind, sometimes moment by moment. Rainbows smile across the hills to gladden the hearts of rain-soaked visitors. Just a glimpse can transform the other reality of Iona – galloping wind, leaden skies and water driven into the pores of your skin. Marvel at the sheep whose sweaters – or jumpers, as they are called there – soak it all in.

The experience of the wild wonder of Iona offers many images to evoke our praise of God …

Nancy Cocks, a former Director of the MacLeod Centre, from Invisible We See You

A soggy sweatshirt, and three sea-smoothed stones

I had been a day visitor to Iona, but it wasn't until a few years ago that I actually got to spend a week on the island. For months I looked forward to spending time in such a powerful 'thin place', hoping to find some new insight for my spiritual journey.

I was especially excited about going on the pilgrimage on the Tuesday. I looked forward to being guided by members of the Resident staff on the seven-mile, five-hour ramble across the island, scrambling across the rocks and bogs and sheep-filled pastures, making stops along the way for a bit of history, a pertinent word about how it all connects to modern life, a bit of prayer – it all sounded perfect.

Ultimately, my most important lesson on that sojourn – in the place where the distance between heaven and earth is tissue-thin, at the time when I was drawn closest to God – had very little to do with history, or prayer, or even the rigorous nature of the hike. For that week, every day I was on the island, it rained. Some days it was just a passing shower, others it was off and on all day. But on pilgrimage day – it was constant.

There were puddles everywhere. At points my boots sunk into mud almost up to my ankles. And by the time I stopped with the others at Columba's Bay to eat my egg-salad sandwich, I was soaked. Despite my waterproof coat, my sweatshirt, my T-shirt, my jeans, my socks and my baseball cap were all drenched. Even my Fruit of the Looms clung to my body!

And so I had a choice. I could choose to be miserable. I could choose to dwell on the fact that the rain was unrelenting, that there was a chill in the air, that my boots were squishing and I was soaked to the skin – or I could simply accept that was how it was going to be and take in the strange beauty of the day as we walked around the island together.

It was in that moment that I realised the divine lesson I was meant to learn on Iona that week. For isn't that often how life works? There are things and circumstances, like rain and muddy boots, that can distract us from really living life fully. There are things that can make us feel miserable. But we can always choose: we can choose to accept those things we can't change for what they are, and instead focus on discovering the good, the true and the beautiful – the things of God, if you will – in each moment of this precious gift called life.

As I left Columba's Bay that day, I picked up three sea-smoothed stones; one of them sits on my prayer table to this very day. And each time I see it, I am reminded to look for God wherever I am, whatever the circumstances in my life. For every place can be a thin place.

John H. Danner

Born again

I first came to Iona in 1958, fresh out of the army from national service. I had been brought up in a Christian tradition which was a mixture of conservative evangelicalism and middle of the road Presbyterianism. Iona blew my mind. A combination of the history of the place – I suppose I had thought that Christianity probably started in Scotland around 1560! – and the excitement of the Iona Community really started me on the road to a new faith. For the first time I met an expression of Christianity that made the link between worship and world, set within the fullness of universal Christianity, in a way that was both accessible and challenging to me. For me, this was like being born again.

John Harvey, a member of the Iona Community, from A Pilgrim's Guide to Iona Abbey

A prayer for those struggling to fulfil their dreams

A prayer by Georgina Shields, a Commissioner of the Poverty Truth Commission and a former Iona volunteer ...

Pray:

- for young carers: for more money and help in the daily struggle ...
- for kids failed by the education system: for more support within school ...
- for all families living in poverty: for food, money and an end to stigma ...
- for all people being discriminated against because of a physical or mental challenge, or because of their religion or beliefs ...

– for The Poverty Truth Commission and all other groups and organisations *'working towards overcoming poverty and ensuring that those affected by decisions are central to decision-making'* ...

– for people who are struggling to fulfil their dreams: pray that their dreams may one day come true ...

Georgina Shields

The spirit in which it is done

I was working in the MacLeod Centre kitchen, the early-morning shift. It was the first time I'd begun the day on my own and the amount of work to be done was daunting. Already two large pans of bread dough were made, the porridge had been cooked and served, and eight dozen scones were cooling on racks. Now it was time to prepare the dozen loaves of bread before the 9.00am worship. As I kneaded and shaped the dough I thought to myself: this baking is all very well – but I would really like to be doing something more spiritual than just cooking day after day.

After setting the bread pans on the cooktops to rise, I rushed down the hill to the Abbey, feeling as though I had done a day's work in a couple of hours.

During worship I was amazed to hear bread mentioned, not once but three times. There was of course: 'Give us today our daily bread' contained in the Lord's Prayer, another reference to bread in the Bible reading, and a third in a song by Bernadette Farrell, 'Christ, be our light':

Longing for food, many are hungry.
Longing for water, many still thirst.
Make us your bread, broken for others,
shared until all are fed.[1]

As I walked back up the hill after the service, light dawned: the making of the 'daily bread' in the MacLeod Centre kitchen was indeed a very spiritual act. It was a small but integral part of the holistic ministry of hospitality. As people sit together at mealtimes they talk and listen, making new friends, sharing their joys, sorrows, struggles, hopes and dreams. For those who live alone, these times of breaking bread together are a particularly important part of the experience of living in community.

Since that time I have spent two more stints in the Abbey and MacLeod Centre kitchens. That early lesson on the importance of breadmaking has stayed with me. Never again has it seemed like a burden but as an opportunity to share, in a very practical way, the love of Christ. It doesn't matter how humble the task: it is the spirit in which it is done which enables transformation from chore to gift.

Lynona Hawkins, South Australia

1. From 'Christ, be our light' © 2013 Bernadette Farrell. Published by OCP

Day 7

A psalm from the Abbey kitchen

Praise the Lord in the chopping of a carrot.
Praise the Lord in the beating of an egg.
Praise the Lord in the frying of onions.
In all our actions, praise you, Lord.

Praise the Lord in the kneading of bread dough.
Praise the Lord in the baking of a cake.
Praise the Lord in the stirring of porridge.
In all our cooking, praise you, Lord.

Praise the Lord in the washing of dishes.
Praise the Lord in the sweeping of the floor.
Praise the Lord in sanitising surfaces.
Let all our work praise you, Lord.

Praise the Lord in the eating of the food.
Praise the Lord in the drinking of our tea.
Praise the Lord in all our grateful graces.
In all our doing, praise you, Lord!

Jennifer Mayston, a former Iona volunteer and an associate of the Iona Community

Day 8

Serving in the Iona Community's shop (Isle of Iona)

I met a man from Montana who came into the shop –
wearing silver chains and bracelets,
fat buckles and leather.

He did his shopping over days
and we got to know one another
in transactions and exchanges.

We spoke about the heavy, wet weather.

About Celtic saints and American cowboys.

About alcohol and brokenness,
as he thoughtfully chose gifts,
which I took and carefully
wrapped up in tissue paper
for his family back home.

About the challenge of living
one day at a time,
and the comfort and strength
of God's love through prayer.

We blessed one another on his last day of purchases and
there was something light and beautiful
in the jangling way he walked out the door:
how he came here like a slave and
sailed off like a song.

George MacLeod spoke of God's great unconditional welcome. Brother
Roger of the Taizé Community wrote: '*To be listened to is the beginning of
the healing of the soul.*'

People came to the Community's shop to spend money of course, to buy
books and souvenirs. Customers also came in with a need to share their
stories, and something of what they had discovered on Iona; to give thanks
to God for time and space to be, and for what they would be taking home
with them. There was sometimes a rich exchange.

With so many people coming to Iona, in the summer especially, it could
sometimes be a real challenge for staff to stay open. Community life was
crowded and busy – life in all its fullness.

After a full day of work and worship, I went home to Cul Dunsmeorach
and wrote the following prayer:

All-embracing, all-loving God,
help me to remain open to the demands
of welcome.

All-accepting, all-seeing Christ,
help me to recognise you in
each tourist and pilgrim.

Holy Spirit
present everywhere always,
enter into me.

Help me to serve
with cheerfulness
humility
gentleness
patience.

Neil Paynter

Day 9

That quiet sunny morning on Iona

In the sad days following my mother's death, my husband and I headed north. One early summer morning we crossed to Iona and strolled along to the Abbey. As we had our little dog with us, she and I perched nearby while my husband went into the church.

The sun was shining. It was quiet and peaceful.

As I sat in the quietness, absorbing the gentle healing of the place, I became aware that I was being asked, 'Why did you think you had to come all this way to find me?' …

Although that was many years ago, the words have stayed with me; have returned to me in anxious and sad times, but in the good times too. And in my mind's eye I gratefully return to that quiet sunny morning on Iona, when I found the answer: 'Perhaps I don't have to, because you are wherever I happen to be.'

Deirdre Hearn

Day 10

God's people

Last Saturday I sat in the Abbey at the welcome service. It was being led by a young woman, a member of the Resident group, with the assistance of other young staff and volunteers. None of them were clergy, none theologically trained, none even on the programme staff. She led a full abbey in worship with such grace, dignity, warmth and sensitivity that I was profoundly moved. The commitment, attention to detail and depth of participation that the service allowed was a model of teamwork by a group of people who had just put in a full and demanding week's work of heavy physical labour. But what struck me most was not just the content, but the integrity of message and medium. In the leadership of God's people in worship with such authority there was a powerful visible sign that God's image is equally to be seen in someone young, female, non-professional, and so we really believe that all are made in God's image ... In the confident leading of singing, of praying, of breaking open the Word by such very young people there was a palpable sense of empowerment. I came away from the service confident that the Spirit still has work for us to do on Iona.

Kathy Galloway, a former Leader of the Iona Community, from Coracle

Day 11

The work of the people

'Liturgy' means 'the work of the people', I'm told. That's how it was on Iona. We all did services – not just the ministers – the cooks, the shop staff, the maintenance team ... Different people had different gifts. Some were good at writing prayers, some were good at music, some were good at leading, some were good at seeing how the whole would hang together … You know, like that bit in Corinthians.

On Iona I felt valued – my life and experience had worth. I didn't have to be a lawyer or a doctor or a pillar of the community to get up in church and tell a story. Iona was a place where people were welcomed, included, challenged, held. I remember one time, ten of us did a service together; it took a week to plan. We wanted to take our time because we really cared about what we were saying.

We got together in a cottage in the evenings after work to plan it. It was so exciting, the way we listened to each other. We were full of dedication and passion. Walking down the road after our meetings the stars seemed close. Some nights I couldn't sleep.

Not everything we did in the service was great – but it was sincere. A lot of it *was* good though – we touched people, moved people, because it was human.

When will the churches change? If liturgy was really 'the work of the people' the churches would be full. What are they afraid of? Losing their jobs?

It's sad really – because there are so many people who are hungry for the spiritual – for more than is being offered in the malls and shops. And to act effectively in the world you need to root yourself, be fed, connect.

The churches don't know what to do to attract people. It seems obvious to me. Iona is a model.

A former volunteer on Iona

Day 12

Where justice and peace embrace

Love and faithfulness are companions: justice and peace embrace.
Faithfulness walks on the earth and justice looks down from heaven.
The children of God will flourish and the land will be fruitful.
Justice will be a sign of the coming Kingdom: the path to it will be peace.
(Psalm 85:10–13, paraphrase)

In Iona this summer I joined a small group of friends who had waited many years to make this pilgrimage together. Nigel and Jill had first come a few years ago, walking several hundred miles from their hometown in Yorkshire. I had joined them for the last few miles, aware that they had much greater stamina, but also blisters and aching knees – and a surge of energy with tears of joy as they stepped off the ferry.

This time they came by car, bringing another friend, Ros, whose journey began in Nigeria, and her carer, Chinonso – a stranger to us who became a friend. These two had never visited the island. With Ros now in a wheelchair, this visit moved at a different pace. Things which were familiar to some of us were seen in a new light through the questions of our companions. From a wheelchair landmarks are seen from a different angle, literally. It was humbling to learn through experience which places were accessible and which not. The statue of the *Fallen Christ* took on a deeper significance when Ros said that falling again and again was, strangely, helping her to journey with God.

For once, there were no long walks over hills or along beaches. Instead we accompanied each other on little expeditions – a stiff push up the brae, a bumpy crossing of grass, a circuit of the cloisters. But in our conversation we ranged through worlds of experience and years spent apart, recalling friends in many places. We shared worship and delight at the way it was a coming-home for some of us, a new-found land for others. Over meals, we talked about the faith that sustains us, our yearning for justice and the way that each of us works for it – connecting sustainable lifestyles and community development in West Yorkshire and Nigeria; caring for the marginalised – those living with leprosy, with mental illness – and learning from them; witnessing injustice in Israel/Palestine while accompanying those who challenge it. Out of our engagement welled up stories; out of our urgent desire for change, tears and laughter. This kind of encounter – the faith that folk bring with them – is one of the things that make Iona holy ground.

Loving God, when we fall your wounded hands lift us up:
you give us companions on a journey, where strangers become friends;
you set our feet on holy ground, where justice and peace embrace –
we give you thanks, wholeheartedly. Amen

Jan Sutch Pickard, a member of the Iona Community, from Walking through Advent

Day 13

Iona: so many stories ...

The date is hazy. The lady's name was Johanna. I'm not sure if she was Dutch or German but she was an inspiring lady, and one story she shared on Iona has really stuck with me. She said once there was a 'down-and-out' blocking her way. She asked to pass. The 'down-and-out' asked for a hug. A passer-by asked her if she was all right. She said she was. Johanna gave the man a hug and he let her pass. Love was shown and they both fulfilled their part of the bargain. I'm sure both were enriched by the interaction. I do find this an inspiring story ...

So many stories ...

Christine Dowling

Day 14

Iona collage (A rainbow time)

The island and the people entwined like some complex Celtic knot –
the weather always an accompanying strand.

Changing colours of the Sound.
Conversations on the road in passing.

Walks in windy silence with new friends –
yellow marsh iris and a shy bird's song.

Sharing a house with an ebb and flow of
colourful, curious world travellers,
ages and surnames never known and just not important.

Learning a new job side by side with thinkers and dreamers:
a gathering of adventurous spirits not knowing what the future holds,
but daring to take the risk –
like Columba and his friends
as they set out across wild, dangerous seas.

Clashes of culture and misunderstandings of humour
requiring a spirit of openness and wonder
at how different we all are
and how similar.

Demonstrating the use of a vacuum cleaner
to a volunteer from a village in Uganda.
Finally the last job finished –
then turning to welcome new arrivals
as the rhythm of a new week begins.

Noticing how folk can both work well together
and avoid each other,
how the ageless challenge of being yourself
with others gives you real opportunities:

to face your fears,
to try to resolve conflict,
to learn to love when it's hard to.

Singing and playing
in an 800-year-old abbey
where words and music mingle and fly,
as workers and pilgrims worship
in their own way.

Recycling and reshaping faiths.
Food for thought,
food for sharing round a table.

Words of wisdom and advice softly spoken
from people who have lived and
learnt from life.

Hot drinks outside –
sitting on a bench with blankets watching the vibrant night sky
shoot stars over your head.

Village hall disco DJing and dancing in your walking boots and jumper,
not giving a toss how you look –
just as long as you're movin' to Marvin's soul.

Ambling over to do a bleary-eyed breakfast shift,
with the early-morning sun awakening over your shoulder.

Beaches and birthdays
with cakes made by a Hungarian confectioner;
handmade cards and thoughtful, crafted presents.

Juggling lettuces down the nave in a children's service:
'Lettuce pray!'

'Bring your thing' coffeehouse nights, with creativity and laughter
and time to talk and meet the new faces.

Sitting in the office
talking to an insomniac Tasmanian Franciscan nun on the phone:
about what's sold in the shop;
describing the day to the other side of the world.

Staffa boat trips to see the painted puffins' clumsy clown arrivals.

Scraping ferry-gate-goodbyes:
struggling to give the meaning of a friendship a final worthy word
or gesture.

A rainbow time:

a group of folk from far and wide suddenly together –
just for a brief time, and then they're gone,
touched by the rain and the sun and each other.
Maybe changed and challenged;
and wondering what's next
and whether
that spirit of togetherness
can be found in another place.

Kath O'Neil, a former Resident group member and volunteer,
from Gathered and Scattered

Iona weaving

How can we comprehend it, God,
this beauty and this pain?
How does it hold together?
Is there pattern or purpose?

On a still December day,
warp and weft glimpsed
in the gold threads of the dawn sky,
in the blue-grey restless waters of the Sound,
in our laughter and our tears,
in our life together in this place –
your mysterious weaving of the world.

In the battle-song and surge of the waves
    and the living silence of the hills.
In the welter of winter gales
    and the sheltering space of the church or home.
In angry exchanges that unravel,
    and words and spaces that heal.
In isolation and in solitude.
In welcomes at the jetty
    and in saying goodbye.
In the wind-bent trees, blasted by salt
    and flowers flourishing in the village gardens.
In busyness that leaves no time
    and folk making time, here and now.
In the richness of all we are given,
    in the ache of all we have lost.

In discord –
　　and in ceilidh music.
Stumbling in the dark –
and dancing under the stars.

How can we comprehend it:
Your beauty and ours – who are made in your image?
Our pain and yours – who chose to share our lives?
We cannot hold it together – but it holds us.

Help us to see pattern and purpose,
　　and our part
in the weaving of the world.

Jan Sutch Pickard, from Out of Iona *(written in part as a blessing of Mhairi Killin's artwork 'Iona weave')*

Day 16

From Paraguay to Iona: a piece of paradise

My name is Rufino Olmedo. I came to Iona in 2004.

When I went to Iona to volunteer it was a big challenge for me. Firstly because I had never been to another country, and also because it was my first time so far away from home. I am from a very little place in the countryside in Paraguay called Santa Maria de Fe.

When you arrive in Iona you do not know anyone – but in a matter of days they become your closest friends.

We were from different places: Germany, England, Scotland, the USA, Poland, Australia, Sweden, Tasmania, Czech Republic, Paraguay …

The weather was very hard for me. Sometimes windy, raining and cold, but this is an island, and a very special one: you're never alone, and so get used to everything.

Mealtime is when you introduce yourself and try to share something about yourself and get to know more about each other.

My favourite time was coffee break, when we shared about our cultures and about our friends, and listened to music from different countries as well as tried different foods.

Life in the community was amazing – working together, singing and praying. When I missed home, I always had someone to support me. I spent time learning lots of wonderful things, and sharing in the church through the Bible and communion. I can also never forget the ceilidh in the village hall, and dancing with my friend Marion.

Life in the community made me stronger in faith. I learnt through sharing with other people regardless of their nationality, denomination, race or other things. Peace and beauty are found in perfect combination in Iona.

If I had another opportunity to go to Iona I would jump at the chance. It is the most magical place in the world and is a piece of paradise. God blessed me in many different ways there. Now I have lots of friends around the world. When I arrived on Iona I never thought that my life would change forever.

Thanks Iona and the people who run the Community, who opened our hearts and made us feel so welcome.

God bless you.

Rufino Olmedo, Santa Maria Education Fund, Paraguay

From Paraguay to Iona: a bag of warm clothes, much tea and some scones

Iona: unique place, unique people – you always want to go back. I'll never forget: I was the only person who was always freezing but they prepared a bag with warm clothes so I could use them. That was very kind of them; I can't explain the feeling.

The island has many grey days – but that did not prevent you from having a nice day at work or a long talk with your roommates – with much tea and some scones.

I remember the delicious food Anja at the Abbey always cooked and taught us to cook. You definitely have to try her meals!

Iona is an amazing place … At one point I thought it would be difficult to stay away from my country for so long. But so many wonderful people made me feel happy, and so today I have such beautiful memories.

I just want to go back.

Noelia Mendoza, Santa Maria Education Fund (http://santamariadefe.org), Paraguay

Day 17

Reilig Oran chapel

This place lies thick with God and centuries
of grief and rage, and plague of kin on kin,
of drownings, famine, emigration, age;
and battles fought by sword, or prayer, and pride,
by monks and warriors, weary hermits, saints
and fishermen, and women working hay.

We come, not to draw back the hardened dead,
whose story's gone beyond their battles' end,
and linger here – behind the warring years
yet touching them, here lies the quiet of Christ.

Here too one night, the air
heavy with the old,
and the waves constant on the shore behind;
here waiting for the silent word
in this place here of peace beneath the fear

there came an instant when the years dissolved
and through the open door a gust of wind
brought back a time long past
when the land lay in innocence,
blessed before the chapel, hermitage or circling grove,
under grey dew, stones and stars,
with the moon glinting upon ancient daisies.

Rosemary Power, a member of the Iona Community

Day 18

Iona moments (from a diary)

… Big Sing in Chapter House with Becky from USA, a Mennonite-trained musician. Sang in Abbey for two services, especially Communion on Thursday evening.

Lots of free time, not too much sitting and listening. Haiku-writing with Steve, painting with Anne. Walks, especially an early-morning one when I met a German lady picking edible leaves.

Biggest (probably) highlight: Steve singing and playing borrowed guitar in Wednesday evening service, unseen in gallery – 'In heavenly love abiding'. Becky adding bits on piano – so beautiful. Also face of Jesus on a flagstone – to my mind anyway – during Sunday morning Communion service.

Chopping vegetables after breakfast each morning in team, including Jackie, who lent Steve her guitar and was thrilled to hear him playing it.

Pilgrimage on Tuesday, so windy at the machair everyone had to stand with backs to it like a lot of penguins and wait for it to stop. Spouting Cave still going.

Silence in Abbey before and after services.

Late-night talk with R and M about R's many suitors before she finally married her husband! M (83) sitting on floor.

Storm on Thursday/Friday morning. Many people leaving in case we couldn't get off island on Friday.

Communion service in choir stalls round long table – wind howling and rattling everything; leader saying to listen to it in our prayers.

Before leaving for ferry, chat with lady from Oxford diagnosed with leukaemia before she came – very positive, and enjoying being here, maybe for last time.

Very special week altogether.

Winifred Wilson

Day 19

At Saint Columba's Bay

At Columba's Bay
they met:
two of Iona's
countless pilgrims.
He, a pastor from Zaire;
she, a broker from Detroit.
And battered by the
autumn wind and rain
they shared their stories –
twentieth-first-century stories –
rooted in contrasting realities,
yet both embedded
in a strange, life-giving
brokenness.

The hidden stories –
of poverty and torture,
of cancer and loneliness;
interweaving stories,
mirroring our
global interconnectedness.

And stories of faith;
of God's unfolding
in their lives
through ordinary days.
And suddenly it seemed

that for a moment
on that distant shore
they glimpsed
that basic truth –
that truly
we are one
in Christ.

Peter Millar, a former Iona Abbey Warden, from An Iona Prayer Book[1]

1. *An Iona Prayer Book*, Peter Millar, Canterbury Press, 1998.
Used by permission of Peter Millar and Canterbury Press

Day 20

Pilgrimage home

I called my mum this evening.
Nothing new, this Sunday ritual.
Long ago, calls became our weekend routine.
Like before, we exchanged greetings,
news, love, what we were doing.
Then, her consistent exclamation:
'Your call has made my day!'
Sadness followed.
Not because our call was brief,
nor due to the distance between us.
No, my mum won't remember this call.
Usually this does not distress me.
For years now, we have shared her Alzheimer's.

Tonight, however, I wanted her to remember Iona.
Iona, place of memory, island of history,
land of deep roots.
I wanted mum to know I was here.
For centuries, pilgrims have come and gone
from this hard and lovely place.
Her pilgrimage is almost over;
she has come to the edge of being gone,
of coming home.
Still her delight when I told her tonight
will be similar to the joy
when I tell her where I am Wednesday,
still here.

Sometimes pilgrims need neither a history
nor a destination.
Sometimes moments of delight suffice.

I came to Iona to learn something.
I did, now I remember,
call home;
that's where all pilgrimages begin.

Ted Bowman, from Fire and Bread

Day 21

Healing and life-giving grace

Living in residential community on Iona or at Camas is certainly an offering that *'does not cost us nothing'*. Constantly making community with one another, and opening up that community to welcome new staff and weekly guests, is a demanding common task. It is hard, conflict is common, and it seems that the very best and the very worst of people comes to the surface. Iona is an exposed place: there is nowhere to hide, least of all from oneself. So, all manner of things can be going on below the surface of the staff group who are serving at table, leading worship, making beds, working in an office or leading programme. Yet, despite all of this, guests have gone away blessed and changed by the experience, and full of praise for the staff team. How does this happen?

I fell to reflecting upon the remarkable experience of grace which guests regularly experience, following a particularly traumatic period within the life of the Resident group on Iona. I was led to Paul's Second Letter to the Corinthians (4:7–10, NIV): *'We have this treasure in jars of clay to show that this all-surpassing power is from God and not from us. We are hard-pressed on every side, but not crushed; perplexed, but not in despair; persecuted, but not abandoned; struck down, but not destroyed. We always carry around in our body the death of Jesus, so that the life of Jesus may be revealed in our body.'*

It dawned upon me that it is not despite such suffering, but because of such suffering, that guests continue to experience healing and life-giving grace.

On Iona, Holy Week and Easter is the opportunity to enter into the drama of the last week of Jesus' life, in order that, having shared in his suffering, we might all the more share in the joy of his resurrection. It is a busy and intense week, with a great deal of preparation going on for the three great days of Good Friday, Holy Saturday and Easter Sunday. So by the Thursday evening, after a difficult management team meeting, I was feeling particularly drained. Biddy (my wife) and I used to find some respite and peace in taking our coffee or tea out to the bench by the infirmary museum from the nearby Warden's flat. Just as I was carrying in the empties, Kathy Galloway, then Leader of the Community, appeared from the Michael Chapel. A former Warden herself, she led and lived through a great many such Holy Weeks on Iona. I blew out my cheeks, and said something about how things felt as if they were falling apart: 'It's always like this,' she said. She reassured me, 'But you'll find that things will resolve themselves over these next three days.'

And she was right. It's as if community life picks up on the betrayals and gossip, the accusations and anger that are part of the story of that first Holy Week. Good Friday dawned red and still, and during the day a peace fell upon us.

Richard Sharples, a former Iona Abbey Warden

Day 22

Misunderstandings in community

Spending 10 weeks in 2000 as a volunteer among 23 others was a most interesting and fulfilling time – many friendships were made.

Each Friday, after the guests had been seen off at the jetty with a Mexican wave, the Resident group and vollies held their weekly meeting. We were asked to decide for ourselves how the meeting was to be conducted; my suggestion one week was that each person took a turn outlining a high or low point of their week.

A Scottish medical student told us *her* highlight was dancing with a young man at the ceilidh … She was fascinated by his job description, which he gave as 'designing metal bras'. In the discussion that followed, we assumed that he was a PhD student involved in researching breast cancer.

A volunteer from Belarus, who had only just started learning English, turned to my Kiwi husband and in a loud voice asked, 'What is a bra?'

Much hilarity ensued as Keith used his hands to attempt to explain the meaning of the word. We think that our friend from Eastern Europe understood!

Helen Weavers, an Iona Community associate living in Australia

Day 23

Re-energised to be on the frontline

I walked there but even if you go by train, take the boat to Mull, then the Iona boat, you begin to feel that you are arriving at the edge of the world … and it's so peaceful, quiet, serene … Iona is pure and if you go with a pure heart your fear, anxiety, anger and pride melts away. These things do not last at Iona. I felt at home at Iona … It's a peaceful place but not a passive place. It's an active place where you can be renewed, invigorated and inspired to communicate with the world. When you go back, whether to Glasgow or London or wherever you come from, to work for transformation, for justice and peace, for equity in the world … all that George MacLeod stood for, you will have new energy and new inspiration. I feel personally that when I went to Iona I was re-energised to be on the frontline.

Satish Kumar, from Coracle

Day 24

The sacrament of meals, music and stories

I volunteered with the Iona Community for the first time during the summer of 2004. I was one of three youth workers at the MacLeod Centre.

What I remember most vividly about my time on Iona are the meals, music and stories.

The smell of fresh-baked bread, homemade soup and Sunday dinners! Meals were a time of nourishment and sacrament, a time of connecting with and serving others – sitting around a table in the MacLeod Centre, passing the bread, serving cups of tea, answering, yet again, the questions: 'Where are you from?' and 'How long have you been here?'

I have very little musical talent, but at worship everyone was taught to sing in parts – and we learned songs from all around the world. I loved the times when worship ended with everyone still singing as we entered the cloisters.

And the stories – walking together on pilgrimages around the island, learning the history of Iona and the Community, listening to gospel dramatisations in worship – and the list goes on.

People often talk about returning to the 'real world' after a week on Iona, but it is the week on Iona that is real. For what really matters is all too easily lost as we go about our daily lives at home, often losing focus on the people around us: those we have the opportunity to serve and those who serve us.

Time spent in community on Iona helps us to remember the sacrament of meals, of voices raised in song and of stories shared from the heart.

Fiona van Wissen

Day 25

Work of human hands

For as long as I can remember, it has been the practice to make the communion bread for Sunday's worship in the Abbey kitchen the day before. It gives a great deal of power to such words in the service as *'fruit of the earth'* and *'work of human hands'* when you know whose hands have made it.

Well, that year we had a gentle giant of a man from North America as a volunteer for six weeks in the kitchen. As the weeks went by, I learned that he was a minister on sabbatical. One of my jobs as Warden was to fill the rota for Sunday morning Communion: Leader, Preacher and Celebrant. So, towards the end of his time as a volunteer, I invited him to be the Celebrant, and he gladly accepted.

Following the service, he told me that he had been approached by an appreciative member of the congregation, who had asked if he was a member of the Community. 'No,' he had delighted to reply, 'I just work in the kitchen.'

Richard Sharples, a former Iona Abbey Warden

Day 26

A bonding that remained for years afterwards

We were a small vigil group in the Oran chapel, with a candle and cross on the floor on Easter eve. A German lady with the voice of an angel led us in a Gregorian chant … The Holy Spirit lifted us up as one.

Something happened during a Christmas visit: there was a bonding that remained for years afterwards. During the guest concert in the Mac common room two young sisters from Atlanta sang 'Little drummer boy', leaving us so moved that most wiped away tears.

I corresponded for several years with a staff member from Romania. She married a pastor at home. I pray she found lasting joy and peace.

One encounter with two talented music teachers from Vienna turned into a real adventure. After chattering away on the pilgrimage, they invited me to Vienna. I went to their school concerts, toured the fabulous music museum, listened to Beethoven in a stunning church setting – and attended an all-night ball in a palace.

My last visit to Iona was with two ladies from Papua New Guinea. Our northbound coach stopped at a Westmorland service station at 3am, but only for a few minutes as we were running late. In Papua New Guinea time doesn't matter. The coach left without them. I was fast asleep. Two soldiers from Edinburgh chased the coach and flagged it down. We sent them engraved whisky glasses from the Abbey shop.

When you go to Iona prepare for the unexpected!

Dick Coates, an associate of the Iona Community

Day 27

Recollections of Iona (particularly Youth weeks in the 1990s)

A thin place, they say.

For me, it has always been about the people. The conversations over soup and bread. A trip to Port Ban with new friends, 'Gordon' by the Barenaked Ladies blaring from an ancient ghetto blaster. Years later, building sand-castles on that same beach, trying to mend a broken heart.

Looking round the platform at Glasgow Central after a sleepless night on a train carriage floor, seeking out fellow Youth week guests. Helping a girl load luggage onto a trolley and meeting a soulmate – the start of an intense friendship that got us both through the loneliness of A-levels.

Losing my best friend after he met the girl of his dreams over an oatcake in the cloisters on the first Sunday; then reuniting on the last night, drying his tears in those same cloisters after he saw her kiss another boy.

Blue porridge. Constant singing. Bells everywhere. Surreptitious hand-holding in the Reilig Oran chapel. Stolen kisses behind the village hall. Tears, a badge of honour at the healing service. Feeling the ghosts of monks at 2am in the Abbey.

Making friends – some for life, some for a season, all precious. Ever connected by an invisible thread. Instantly tripling the number of people to say hello to at Greenbelt. Taking drastic action, in those days before mobile phones or Facebook, to feed those friendships and relive the Iona experience. A week after passing my driving test, travelling 65 miles on my own just to see Iona friends for an evening. Discovering connections years later: my best friend's Abbey roommate marrying a girl I met at Student week. A Glaswegian lad from Youth week 1994 turning up at a Holy City planning group meeting. And so it goes on.

Coming home and devising ways to combat PIDS (Post-Iona Depression Syndrome). Drinking endless cups of tea. Buying oatcakes from Waitrose. Playing Debussy's 'Clair de lune' on the piano in my dining room and hearing it echo round the Abbey. Fighting the urge to respond: 'We will seek peace and pursue it' or 'Offerings that cost us nothing' at random intervals. Baking Iona Abbey bread while singing 'Uyai mose'. Knowing that nothing would ever be quite the same again.

Decades later, most of the friendships are long gone but Iona's legacy lives on. I moved to Edinburgh and stayed for 20 years. My Iona connections are still leading me to meet some of the most wonderful, fascinating and challenging people. I still have the pebble given to me at Youth week 1993. The Clark tin whistle a friend bought at the Abbey shop for my 18th birthday is still in use. I gave out pebbles from Columba's Bay as wedding favours so that all our friends and family would have a piece of Iona for themselves.

A small Scottish island with a reach around the world.

Caroline Spratt, an associate of the Iona Community

Day 28

Soul-opening

I first made the journey to Iona in 1979. Like so many of my generation, I mistook what people said about God *for* God, and found most of what I heard in church hypocritical or irrelevant to the new world, free from superstition and guilt, which I was sure we would inaugurate. As a young lesbian, the message I had received from my childhood faith community was that there was no place for me at God's table. So I defiantly decided to find a new place of sustenance with a different menu.

I was travelling around Britain alone and had been quite bored with London. On what seemed like a whim, I decided to take the train to Edinburgh. I wasn't prepared for the beauty that unfolded the further north I went. I saw huge swathes of land stripped down to bare rock and scrub – marvels of tenacity and survival. I was moved and ill at ease in ways I didn't fully understand.

While spending time on Skye, I heard some fellow travellers talking about an island called Iona. So when I got off the ferry from Oban it was as a bored tourist unaware that it would be the first leg of a spiritual journey of profound diversity and richness.

It was on Iona that I first became acquainted with the medieval Christian monastics called *peregrini* and the wisdom of the Celtic church. I resonated with those wanderers and found my story within theirs as I navigated troubled waters and finally acknowledged my long-denied spiritual yearning.

My second trip to Iona was in 1995 as a second-year divinity student. Standing in the bow of the ferry facing the bitter cold wind, I knew that this visit would be very different. No longer a timid and troubled tourist, I was free to give myself over to the spirit of the island. As I sat quietly in the Abbey church I allowed myself to see and feel the stones as transmitters of thousands of prayers, expressions of fear and hope, including my own. Looking with new eyes across the magnificent blue of St Columba's Bay I felt a profound connection with the sea, the sand, the birds and all of God's glorious creation.

In the 37 years since that first visit, I continue to navigate troubled waters – a lifelong task for anyone who is truly awake and engaged in this suffering world. As I enter my elder years I reflect that the gift Iona gave that young woman all those years ago was a soul-opening – enabling me to embrace myself and all of creation as beautiful. I have also come to see that there is infinite variety at God's table and to know that I always have a place there. This *peregrinus* has come home.

Sandra Malasky, New Brunswick, Canada

Day 29

The ferry

I've a love-hate relationship with the CalMac ferry.

There's that wonderful feeling of anticipation of leaving your car, and what people call civilisation, at the car park; then waiting for the grind of the ferry-flap as it settles onto the Fionnphort slipway; then walking onto it, and leaning on the starboard side to get a better view of the Abbey, the swish of water, white beneath, and then … then the different flap-noise as it clangs onto Iona concrete and one steps mindfully onto the land that called you.

'Life is all about beginnings and endings, and more new beginnings,' I tell myself … as I do a week later, lifting my foot off Iona soil and both feet onto that dratted ferry again. There's no way I can grasp the truth of that catchy mantra at this point. All I can do is to lean on that same (now port side) ferry, and weep.

Why, oh why, do the tears flow – every single time? Annoying tears, real tears. But those tears, I have realised, tell me, again and again, that I have touched the golden thread.

I weep often, this man in his seventies; and I know it's my personal marker showing me, reminding me, that the Spirit is still alive within.

Maybe the ferry is my St Christopher, carrying me, holding me – whichever direction it's moving. And maybe it doesn't matter anyway, as long as I'm held.

Paul Heppleston, an associate of the Iona Community

Day 30

Iona dance

Somehow the air seems to dance differently here,
executing a perfect back-flip into the arms of the short-cropped hillsides,
gliding in sequinned splendour and perfect three-four time
across the machair,
juggling with rooks and tossing them ragged
into the raw wind,
swaying, arms entwined, with the green flags
and the surprised white daisies,
somersaulting spectacularly over the cotton grass,
jitterbugging with the spray and
jiving with the spinning sun-specks
over the water,
tapping in time with the tip-tapping pebbles
as they partner the dinner-jacketed oyster-catchers,
line dancing on the telephone wires
to the hum of other people's messages,
smooching in a long, last waltz with the silver sands …
somehow, here, the air just dances.

Alix Brown, a member of the Iona Community, from This Is the Day

Day 31

At least once in your life ...

Take a crazy diversion
Visit the top of a mountain
Be storm-swept by wind and rain
Sleep under the stars

Sing
Smell the blossom as spring arrives
Open your mouth and catch raindrops
Lie down and watch

      satellites cross space

Stand under a tree and look up
In a rock pool and look down
Sit by a beach fire till it burns to embers
Spend time in your own company
Listen to the sound of waves through a window

Discover love
Discover silence

Fiona Caley, a former Iona Resident group member and an associate of the Iona Community, from Around a Thin Place

Month

Four

Day 1

Engaged spirituality

You might think spirituality is the opposite of worldliness. In a sense it is, for it is neither materialistic nor earthbound. Its language is imaginative and poetic. It comes from the heart and speaks to the soul. Its kingdom is not of this world. So people tend to pursue it in places far removed from their everyday lives.

Yet it was on Iona, the most remote place in which I have ever lived, that I came across the expression 'engaged spirituality'. And engaged spirituality is certainly not about getting away from it at all. Or if it is, it is about getting away just long enough to be propelled back into the thick of it.

Engaged spirituality goes to the very heart of Christianity. To the Incarnation. To God revealed amid the ordinariness and suffering of our world. In Jesus. In all human life. In everything God has made and called good. If it takes a remote island to bring this home to us, that's fine – provided we *do* take it home.

Whatever it is that drives so many pilgrims to this ancient Hebridean island, Iona Abbey offers no escape route from the conflicts of the world. Its worship continually focuses on the issues of our lives and times. It also focuses on God of course, but that is not necessarily so different. The line between heaven and earth can be very thin there. Because the island is a heavenly place, some say. But also because the Iona Community has a particularly earthy view of the Faith. Its members are dispersed around the country and in other parts of the world, connecting work and worship, prayer and politics, as they try to rebuild community.

As George MacLeod saw Iona Abbey gradually returning to its former glory, he put it this way in one of his prayers:

Take us outside, O Lord, outside holiness,
out to where soldiers curse and nations clash
at the crossroads of the world.
So may this building be justified.

Brian Woodcock, a former Iona Abbey Warden, from Holy Ground

Day 2

The journey from Iona to South Africa and back

In 2003 I journeyed to Iona from South Africa. I was at a crossroads in my life and needed time to reflect on the way ahead, but also excited about coming home to my own country and folk.

I was invited to lead a peace and justice service in the Abbey. I used Archbishop Desmond Tutu's book *There Is No Future without Forgiveness*, in which there is the story of Amy Biehl, who was a Fullbright scholar from California attached to the University of the Western Cape, and who, over a long period, had been involved in the anti-apartheid student campaign. On August 25, 1993 she gave a lift to some student friends, taking them into Gugulethu township. Youths stoned the car, and when Amy and her passengers got out, the mob chased them and stabbed Amy. She, who was committed to justice, was killed by the people whose cause she espoused.

Her family were shattered. Yet instead of being embittered and seeking revenge, Amy's parents attended the amnesty hearing of the Truth and Reconciliation Commission; and in fact embraced the families of the murderers of their child. What was more remarkable is that they established the Amy Biehl Foundation (www.amyfoundation.co.za) with the objective of uplifting the youth in the very township where their daughter was killed.

Out of the blue, on my return to South Africa, I met the chairperson of the

Foundation. I was challenged to present workshops to their team of facilitators, who went into the townships to work with young people on various projects. I was invited to tell stories to the children in the dusty schools of the townships – and to enjoy their energy and laughter. I discovered that two of the young men who were part of the group responsible for Amy's death were now involved in the Foundation.

For me the journey from South Africa to Iona, and back, held the message that *'there is no future without forgiveness'*. On Iona I had to learn through prayer what work this commitment required of me.

Muriel Connell, an associate of the Iona Community,
who has recently returned to Scotland after 40 years in South Africa

Day 3

Address to a pilgrim

Rome to Canterbury
Derry to Iona
Iona to Bamburgh
Bamburgh to Bradwell
Whitby to Whithorn –
pilgrimage is a circular route,
following the scuffmarks of history.
Beware the onslaught of nostalgia,
look out for sickly sentimentality,
the saintly monk who never broke a fingernail
or into sweat.
Remember, rather, and walk
in the footsteps of countless refugees,
tramping the forests of fear,

camping out in the fields of hopelessness;
the scent, not of crushed myrtle, but panic,
the sound, not of the lark, but of the sniper's bullet,
soaring, seeking warm flesh.

Seek then to remember
the brave steps of Mandela,
the unfinished work of Luther King,
the courage and compassion of Romero.
Carry with you also herstory:
Margaret of Scotland and Hilda of Whitby;
Clothilde and Bertha, persuasive princesses;
Elizabeth Fry and Emily Pankhurst,
who broke open prisons and set free prisoners.

Remember all the invisible ones;
walk in the footmarks of the forgotten ones.
And when your place of departure
becomes also your place of arrival
and you 'know the place for the first time'*
what has changed?
What have you indulged?
In seeking have you been found?
In penance have you travelled
the long hard road to restitution?
And as you step off and out of the procession,
what of you will those who continue
carry until you meet again?
What of them do you bring to us?

Kate McIlhagga, from The Green Heart of the Snowdrop

* T.S. Eliot

Day 4

A shared and very marvellous experience:
Kinship Carers group on the MB Iolaire

Over the last two decades Davie and I have run trips from Iona to the Isle of Staffa on our boat the *MB Iolaire of Iona*. We love doing this and every day is enjoyable with something remarkable happening.

Every Monday and Wednesday we have guests from the Abbey and MacLeod Centre. The system is very efficient and I usually receive a phone call the night before with numbers for the boat. On the next day the passengers arrive at the pier and are taken out on an adventure to see Fingal's Cave and sometimes puffins.

After these folk leave the jetty a member of staff usually comes to Tigh-na-Traigh and we have a bit of a catch-up and a blether. On one of these occasions the staff member told me that there would be no group on the next usual day, although there were guests in the Mac. She explained that perhaps they might not manage such a long trip as they were unfamiliar with boats and the sea. There were youngsters as well as older people. They belonged to the Kinship Carers group from Glasgow and many had been living under difficult circumstances.

I suggested they come down at 5pm when Davie was finished with his usual run, as I was sure he would take them out on the boat to give them at least a chance to experience it.

This is what happened:

A group of adults and young children appeared, and I thought they were all very quiet. They boarded. Since it wasn't too rough I decided to take my three-year-old grandson, Finn, aboard too. Finn likes the *Iolaire* but he likes people more and was full of smiles directed at everyone on board. His little golden head bobbed up and down as he offered out his strawberries to share. Some of the wee ones on board were a bit shy. There were a few grannies and some really young children. We set off. Finn managed to inveigle a place beside a wee girl of similar size up at the stern of the boat, positioned on the red carpet. He chattered away in his gobbledegook way.

As we crossed the Sound the waves got bigger. We were heading for Erraid, hopefully to see the seals there. I think the folk were quiet because they were nervous. Then one wee boy shouted out: 'We are going to sink!' as he looked over the stern at the waves. There was a general air of tension after that. As we sailed towards Tinker's Hole we spotted a couple of seals on the rocks. Everyone drew their attention to these dark lumps sprawled on the distant boulders. They were quite impressed and forgot about sinking for a while. It was soon time to turn and go home and people were starting to relax.

All of a sudden, as we left to cross back to Iona, there was a splash and then a flash of something shiny and grey. The water around frothed up as dolphins came alongside the boat keeping pace, diving under the bow and jumping and cavorting around the *Iolaire*. There were lots of them.

Everyone, young and old, let out collective sighs of wonder. It was a great moment and all were smiling, laughing, pointing and just enjoying the company. The dolphins didn't disappoint and seemed to be joining in with it all. I have been aboard often and seen many things but the atmosphere and the dolphins at play that evening was outstanding.

All too soon we were back at the pier ready to get off. As one wee boy left the boat he turned and shouted to Davie, 'Thanks, Mister, for getting the dolphins to come for us!'

I had a job persuading the ladies on board that the privilege had been ours, for without them, as well as the dolphins, we would not have had that shared and very marvellous experience.

I'd like to say how much Davie and I have enjoyed carrying Iona Community guests to Staffa. We have made many very good friends, whom we cherish, and have been honoured to provide this service.

Carol Kirkpatrick of Staffa Trips, Iona (www.staffatrips.co.uk)

Conversation with a stone at St Columba's Bay

Amidst the crash and bluster of the seaside, a dip in the wind, a break in the clouds. I stop and breathe in deeply, tasting the salt and warmth and silence of the moment.

'Hey,' I hear, 'would you mind moving? You're blocking my sun!'

I look around. A jiggle, a tumble.

A stone nudges my foot.

'I said,' says the stone, 'could you step aside a little? The sun won't be out long and I'd like to enjoy it.'

A stone? Said? I move aside, wishing to be polite, though deeply confused.

I crouch down and take a closer look.

'Is that … better?' I ask.

'Yes, thank you,' comes the reply.

And with that I am in conversation with a stone. We talk through the blustery afternoon.

I tell her of my life … She tells me of the events and forces that have shaped her.

'My journey has been long,' she concludes.

'Mine as well,' I say.

'Not so far as mine,' responds the stone. 'You still have rough bits.'

Alec W McTavish

The natural cross

It was three months after my husband's heart operation that I reached Iona, travelling with a group of other German women. It was my deepest wish to stay once for a full week at the Abbey.

During the first night I couldn't sleep. So I got up, at 2am, and went into the Abbey. I sat in the middle of the church, staring at the silver cross on the communion table and thinking about the past weeks and the events of the night of my husband's heart attack. He had been closer to death than life. Finally, after 30 minutes – and during my prayers not to be left a widow with two still-dependent children – one of the medical assistants said the magical sentence: 'He is coming back.' …

The following weeks had been hard but I always got enough power to arrange all the needed things, but myself felt without power and exhausted. My main task was to be confident when I visited my husband in the different hospitals or talked with my children. During the first weeks I planned to cancel the journey to Iona, but a voice told me to wait.

Now I was sitting in the Abbey and feeling deeply thankful. After a prayer of thanks, I went back to bed and slept much better.

During my stay I often went into the Abbey during the lonely late nights for a prayer by the silver cross.

One day during the week the craftworker at the MacLeod Centre showed us how to make a natural cross from things collected on Iona.

So on pilgrimage day I collected two pieces of driftwood for the cross itself, shells, a piece of fishing net, a root, sheep's wool from a fence, feathers, flowers, a piece of fern, some green marble for decoration, and a big flat stone for the base.

Back at home in Germany I put all these things together. I feel the power and spirit of Iona every day while sitting and praying in front of this cross.

Thanks to God and Iona.

Jutta Tripp, a member of the Iona Community in Germany

Day 7

To get to Iona

To get to Iona
it takes me
the Underground
three trains
a coach
two ferries
and a fair bit of walking.

To get to Iona
it takes me
sandwiches
coffee

sweets
a bottle of water
and sometimes
on the boat
an egg-and-bacon butty.

To get to Iona
it takes me
timetables
The Guardian quick crossword
a book
a pen and some paper
and whatever magazines
people leave behind them
on the trains.

To get to Iona
it takes me
smiles
conversations
laughter
listening
memories
and often tears.

To get to Iona
it takes me
risks
prayers
work
wonder
minutes and days
and the passing of years.

That's what it takes me
to get to Iona.

What will it take you?

Ruth Burgess, a member of the Iona Community, from Around a Thin Place

Day 8

A place of hope

'A place of hope,'
they say:
and in their thousands
they journey, year by year,
to this tiny island
on the margins of Europe.
Sunswept and windswept,
yet always deeply
a place of transformation.
A sacred spot on earth:
a pilgrim's place
of light and shadow
energy and challenge.

We need you, Iona,
with your alternative vision,
with your ever-present questions
your often uncomfortable silence.
For you are a place of prayer,
of Christ's abiding:
weaving a rainbow of meaning

through the endless busyness of our days,
holding together the frayed threads
of our fleeting devotion,
opening a path for healing
and for peace.
Not momentary healing
nor easy faith,
but struggle, commitment,
and an ongoing conversion
are your gifts for
our broken yet beautiful lives.

Peter Millar, a member of the Iona Community, from An Iona Prayer Book[1]

1. *An Iona Prayer Book*, Peter Millar, Canterbury Press, 1998. Used by permission of Peter Millar and Canterbury Press

Day 9

A modern-day parable

The way to Iona entails driving about 30 miles across the Isle of Mull. While catching the ferry from Oban on the Scottish mainland, forewarnings are given about allowing at least an hour to cross Mull to reach the other ferry to Iona.

The road is single track and the quality of the journey is determined by one's temper and the equanimity of other drivers. It would not be sensible for two vehicles to pass one another on the road for the edges of the tarmac can be some inches above the soft verges. There are lay-bys which occur every so often on either side of the road. On a hilltop, it is possible to see a vehicle like a dinky toy in the distance so that one can wait in a passing place, but with sudden bends and drops in the road, there are other occasions requiring quick decision-making. The next passing place becomes an essential if from behind comes a delivery man who thinks you should be getting a move on. It's too bad if the space is occupied by a bus or cars awaiting other travellers coming the other way.

But the whole experience is enlightened by others: those eager to give right of way, the acknowledgement of thanks for consideration and the recognition that we are all dependent on one another.

Our travel in faith is called 'the way'. Jesus said, 'I am the way, the truth and the life.'

I found the journey across Mull similar to our faith, with its pleasures and problems, some expected, others thrust upon us, the resting places for reassessment, the heights with long views, the valleys which have their own beauty to be recognised, and most importantly, the companionship, or otherwise, of people travelling the same road.

Jesus spoke of 'the way', but this road needs lay-bys too. Is that where prayer and contemplation come in, helping us to reach the truth and the life?

Geoff Prestage

Day 10

'You journey to Iona three times'

I recently began volunteering with an organisation called 'We Grow Together', which teaches children about gardening and eating local, in-season food. It felt like a gift, and I know my time on Iona, working in the kitchen and with the programme team, contributed to my transition. I went from working in a cubicle at a national magazine in New York City to baking bread and working in food and health, and even music (staff choir got me back into singing). Life is certainly a journey …

I was told a few different things about Iona: the first was that 'you journey to Iona three times'; the second was that people claim they found Iona 'by accident' (but it's no accident); and the third was that no one is meant to stay forever: we have to return to the world and use what we learned on Iona to make the world a better place.

My first awareness of Iona came when my mother threw a magazine on my bed containing an article about pilgrimage trips with John Philip Newell. I wasn't a very religious person; I called myself spiritual. So when the itinerary for the trip arrived in my e-mail inbox, I was a bit nervous when I saw all the Abbey worship times listed. You see, I had blindly signed up for the workshop not really researching Iona, its past or function as a spiritual Mecca. I still got on the plane, and the train, and the ferry, and the bus, and the other ferry, that late October day in 2009.

That was the starting point of a new chapter in my life, though I didn't know it at the time. My New York existence had started showing cracks; but the city me was still ready to leave the unaccustomed quiet of Iona by the end of the week, though when I returned to the States, I realised something inside me had changed. I had taken my first steps as a pilgrim, and on the Iona pilgrimage had thrown my first stone into St Columba's Bay: an action of releasing the old parts of me.

These lessons followed me into my daily life. And I returned to Iona in 2011 for another week as a guest. By this time, my urban self had unravelled completely and I knew I was ready to cross the threshold into a new life chapter. When I returned home, I submitted an application to volunteer with the Iona Community. I was on my way.

In May 2012 I quit my entire old life to be a kitchen volunteer at the Abbey. I had become a herbalist and cook in my time between Iona visits and wanted to gain experience in cooking for large groups in a 'retreat' setting. My stay was transformative, not only as a cook, but as a human being. I met, worked and worshipped with people from around the world and found a groundedness and rawness that went so deep. I couldn't imagine myself being anywhere else. But I had to leave (as I'd been told).

Upon returning to the States, my Iona withdrawal pointed me towards culinary and health coaching school. I was invited to stay with a fellow vollie while attending school (one of the many kindnesses I have experienced from my Iona family), and am in the process of fusing my new skills into ways to help people in need. I still use my breadmaking skills! My three times to Iona were a magical turning point in an ever-unfolding journey.

Lee Ann Monat

Day 11

A gift I brought home with me

Iona was a name that had been a part of my consciousness for a very long time. After graduating from university, I went to teach at a high school in Ocho Rios, Jamaica, named, you guessed it, Iona. It never occurred to me to ask the headmaster why a school in Jamaica had been named after an island across the Atlantic. Through the years, I heard colleagues speak about study-leave time spent on Iona; and at some point someone introduced me to Iona's worship resources, which I have been using ever since.

After so many years of hearing and dreaming about the place, as the train pulled out of Glasgow Queen Street Station and headed north, I had to pinch myself. Everything had finally fallen into place and I was on my way.

I had signed up for a week at the MacLeod Centre. At first I was disappointed not to be staying in the Abbey; but it turned out to be a blessing as there was a delightfully diverse group of thirty people at the Mac from six countries and seven denominations.

The coursework was good, but to be honest, it was the relationships with the community of people that I cherished. For one week a group of folk from all around the world came together to live, work, pray, hike, worship, dance, talk, drink tea and laugh together.

I had gone to Iona without expectations, apart from learning why this one place drew so many people, including myself.

There was no thunderbolt spiritual experience for me that week. Instead I found the beauty of the landscape, worshipping in the quiet of the Abbey, the pilgrimage around the island and getting soaked in a chilly rain, even cleaning the MacLeod Centre with other people – that these experiences of everyday life were what touched my soul. It was such a change from my life filled with expectations. At Iona I did not have to accomplish a thing. No one needed anything from me. I could simply let the week evolve. I could spend time listening to another person's story. I could sit and gaze at the sea or watch a bird circling in the sky. I could simply be a part of God's world and be in God's presence. This is a gift I received on Iona that I brought home with me.

Carol Reed

Day 12

On the road

I was a pilgrim
that summer
I went to Iona.

I slept in a tent
worshipped in an abbey
walked under stars.

I saw and heard God
in many new ways.

I went home
feeling good.

I went on living,
meeting God in new ways
in old places.
I was surprised.

Being a pilgrim
does something to you
that changes you forever.

It puts you
on the road
with God.

Ruth Burgess, a member of the Iona Community, from Around a Thin Place

Day 13

It didn't smell natural

A few years ago on Iona, I met a woman in her seventies who shared with me the story of her spiritual journey. She had grown up in the southern United States. It was her family's custom to attend church every Sunday. One particular Sunday morning nearly sixty years ago, she was sitting in church when, halfway through the liturgy, a dog wandered into the sanctuary. It sauntered up the central aisle, sensing its way forward, until it got to the altar. There it stopped and began to sniff around. No, it did not do what you think I am going to say! It turned around and left. It did not like what it smelled. 'That is when I left the church,' the woman said to me. 'It didn't smell right. It didn't smell natural.'

It was a dog that guided this woman to see as a young adolescent that her religious environment did not smell right, that it had lost the connection between the natural and the holy, between spirit and matter, between God and creation. Her experience is eccentric in its details but it is the story of countless numbers of women and men in the Western world today. They too have been born in the Christian household. They too no longer come to the family table. And it is because they too have not been truly nourished there in the past. Intuitively, they have known within themselves the goodness of the natural, the sacred origin of what is deepest in our nature and in all nature. Yet in so many cases, not only has that longing been neglected, but the religious fare they have been offered contradicts some of their deepest knowing and hunger for the goodness of creation.

John Philip Newell, from Christ of the Celts

Day 14

The possibility of being open and vulnerable

I led a week on Iona with Steve Whiting, a long-time colleague and friend working for Quaker Peace and Social Witness in London. Our focus for the week was the commemoration of the pain, suffering and sacrifice of people during the First World War, but also included reflections on all wars, and folk's endeavours to work for peace. It was necessarily a hard topic and some of it was indeed unbearable, but, as is the way in Iona, our programme was very varied and creative. We studied and discussed some pretty harrowing first-hand material from diaries and letters from World War One; we participated in a hilarious role play which revealed a great deal about disinformation, propaganda and the many dilemmas of conflict; we sang songs of war and peace; and we listened to a fascinating presentation about the effects of WWI on composers and musicians. And, of course – we talked, argued and discussed. All this amid the beauty of Iona in the best of summer weather. As one participant said: 'The island itself creates safety and the possibility of being open and vulnerable.'

And it was this openness and vulnerability which enabled one of the finest sessions of the week. On the Wednesday evening we gathered round very informally in the Mac common room, seated on cushions and chairs, for a storytelling session. There was no set order, but as each personal story or memory of war was told, others followed naturally and a pattern emerged. People shared their experiences at a very deep level and we were all profoundly moved …

Helen Steven, from Coracle

Day 13

A zebra, tiger, monkey, giraffe and gorilla in the Iona village hall

Recently at Camas (the Iona Community's Adventure Centre on Mull) we welcomed a fantastic group from the Provanmill/Blackhill area of Glasgow.

Many of the young people and leaders had been before – and were very excited to be back. As soon as the group arrived, they changed straight into their impressive assortment of animal onesies!

As the group had been before they had already achieved the first level of the John Muir Award. So this time they aimed to take on the Explorer part of the award, which linked in with nature walks done on their first day at Camas, where the group walked to Trig Point. The walk was really enjoyable – though we nearly lost two of the group to the 'Bogness Monster', as they went waist-deep into the bog. Another great moment was one young person standing on the hill shouting famous lines from *Braveheart*! We even camped on Iona, and went to the Monday night ceilidh. The group arrived in their assortment of onesies, which included a zebra, tiger, monkey, giraffe and gorilla all dancing away to 'Strip the Willow' in the Iona village hall ...

From the Camas Diary (the Camas blog)

Day 16

Into the light

Iona
creeps up on you
round a corner in Mull.
The jetty
the Abbey
Dun I
and the village.
Such an insignificant sight
to bear the weight of history.
So small a place
to be crammed full
of visions and memories.
Beloved isle
bewitching place
of saints and sinners
strangers
and the well-known ones.

Laid flat at sunset
on a calm sea.
To walk to the North End
is to walk off
the edge of the world.
To enter the womb
of the Abbey at evening
is to receive a calm
a blessing,

then to be
expelled
into the light.

Kate McIlhagga, from The Green Heart of the Snowdrop

Day 17

An Iona Christmas

There's a 'house party' on Iona at Christmastime. Volunteers come from all over the world to welcome guests, some of whom have been going through very tough times all year.

I remember a gathering we had once in the Abbey common room, following Communion in the Michael Chapel, at the end of one of those weeks.

It was like the whole world was in that room – folk from America, Poland, Wales, Pakistan …

Charles was talking to Stuart. Charles was from Hampstead Heath and Stuart was from Possilpark. Stuart had needed to get away from where he was staying for a bit, to steer clear of the temptation of drugs and drink. Stuart and Charles had seemed worlds apart. They'd barely understood each other's accents. Had trouble carrying on a conversation around the table at mealtimes at first.

Joan was strumming Christmas carols on her acoustic guitar – and TJ was singing. Joan described herself as 'a radical feminist singer-songwriter/ecowarrior priestess'; TJ played American football. He had a soft and gentle voice; subtle phrasing. There'd been some ups and downs in the week (as usual) and at one point TJ and Joan had shouted and screamed at each other in the middle of community chores. Now they were sitting together making music:

'It came upon the midnight clear,
that glorious song of old,
from angels bending near the earth
to touch their harps of gold ...'

In many ways it was like the end of any typical week on Iona. Pauline and Maggie were talking to Sofija and Pristina, who were volunteers. Pauline and Maggie were sisters. Their ninety-three-year-old mother had died in September and they'd come to Iona for Christmas because they used to come to Iona with their father and mother when they were girls. It was a place where they had both felt happy: something they had in common. I glanced round the common room. Stuart and Charles were exchanging addresses and e-mails now. Later, I saw the sisters sitting together in the cloisters, watching the first snowflakes fall, clouds of their breath and cigarette smoke mingling in the air.

'Thanks. I've never *had* a good Christmas,' Stuart said to me going out into the night.

'... when peace shall over all the earth
its ancient splendours fling,
and all the world give back the song
which now the angels sing ...'

I went outside, in back of the Abbey; there was moonlight on the sea and I gazed up at the stars. I could see an announcement in the sky: It said that the whole world could be reconciled: brothers from Possil and Hampstead Heath, women and men, neighbours from the Balkans, estranged sisters ...The world had travelled to the 'world island' of Iona to come together and be touched and healed. And the Earth is an island in the sea of the universe, I thought. A common room in God's many-roomed mansion.

And I closed my eyes and breathed in the stars and earthy night ...

When I left Iona I took that announcement back. It's harder to see the stars on the mainland, with the pollution, interference, glare ... Sometimes I walk out to the country-dark to remember that night. Sometimes I need to come all the way back to Iona to be reminded of infinite possibilities.

There's neither rich nor poor,
male nor female:
All are one in Jesus Christ.

Neither black nor white,
First World nor Third World:
All are one in Jesus Christ.

No 'radical feminist singer-songwriter/eco-warrior priestess',
no conservative American football player:
All are one in Jesus Christ.

No ex-junkie living in a park,
no cocaine addict wandering lost on a heath:
All are one in Jesus Christ ...

Turn off your TV screen that breeds fear
and go outside
and gaze up at the awesome sky
full of promise ...

Breathe in the stars
smell the night.
Christ is born today
and every day ...

Neil Paynter, from Good News of Great Joy

Day 18

Watchnight service prayer from Iona

God with us –
as the wind comes rushing through the darkness
across miles of wild ocean
and batters this building,
as the gales howl through the gaps
and hurl sleet against the windows,
we know that we are held safe,
out of this raging and wrathful world
in a sheltering place,
as though in the hollow of your hand:
strong and caring God.

God with us –
we know, too, that you are present
in the power of creation:
the energy of wind and water,
the majesty of Ben More crowned with snow,
the mystery of the night sky,
the intricate beauty of a shell.
On a day like this
we feel the beat of your heart;
on a night like this
we are so close, we hear you breathing,
and we are inspired, caught up in your life:
strong creative Spirit.

God with us –
on a day like this,

on a night like this;
in a place like this,
in a world like this –
a world of suffering and hope,
of tears and laughter –
at the turning of the year
we turn to you.

Jan Sutch Pickard, a member of the Iona Community, from Hay and Stardust

Day 19

Iona visitors

They come on days
so grey the sea may
heave them to shores they waited
years to see;
or come of curiosity
to pay brief praise
where old monks prayed,
and raised the cross
in stillness.

Where once they stayed
the heritage remains
and those who wait
listening may hear,
sounding through pilgrim time
and grace-loved centuries,
they tread again on holy ground.

Rosemary Power, a member of the Iona Community

Day 20

Setting out

We got up while it was still dark
and gathered in Cul Shuna*
to say goodbye to Martina,
Kieran,
Maya,
Rahim,
Sarah and Maggie,
Jack and Dot and
Billy.

We held a service in the living room
out of the *Iona Abbey Worship Book*.
During the prayers we gave thanks to God for our time together
and asked Jesus to be with everyone on the road.
In silence we held hands …
then sang 'Sent by the Lord am I'.

At breakfast,
Kieran was saying that he would be working in a homeless shelter
in Glasgow.

Maggie said she was going back to school
to be a midwife.

Dot and Jack were opening a house of welcome for asylum seekers
and refugees.

I asked Billy what he was going to do.
He said he wasn't sure,
it hadn't really dawned on him yet –

but he knew it would,
in time.

He'd follow his heart.
He'd learned to do that here,
follow his heart.
It was the same as following Jesus, Billy said.

Helen called that the ferry was coming!
We ate our toast on the run.
Someone said:
Jesus was already on the ferry.
Kieran said, No –
he was probably halfway to Glasgow by now!

At the jetty we hugged and
said we'd keep in touch –
the air was salty,
seabirds cried –
it felt like hell.

The ferry pulled away –
we stood in a long line
and did the Mexican wave.

Our friends waved back.
Billy blew us a big kiss – and we all laughed.

Then gradually

in ones
and twos
and threes

Martina and
Kieran and
Maya and
Rahim and
Sarah and Maggie and
Jack and Dot
and Billy
turned to face the sunrise
coming up
over the mountains of Mull.

Neil Paynter, from Iona Dawn

* A house in the village

Day 21

The story of an electrician

The story of an electrician who came with us to Iona demonstrates the objective nature of healing power. He was mainly concerned with the rebuilding of Iona Abbey, but during the healing service he found himself carried forward to the front and sharing in the laying on of hands. Afterwards he came to me saying: 'What's all this? When I laid my hands on that woman's head I felt electricity. I am an electrician, and I know electricity. I don't understand all this holy stuff.' We explained as best we could, and through this he came to be a man of real faith who leads a healing service in his parish church each week, conducting a quiet but effective lay ministry.

Ian Cowie, from Jesus' Healing Works and Ours

Day 22

A sceptic healed?

A healing service has always been a troublesome idea for me. After all, as a hospital consultant, don't I work in the 'healing service'? Isn't that a 9 to 5 job, surrounded by the paraphernalia of modern medicine? In my case, particularly my microscope, where I can see how disease happens and in most cases why. I can tell my clinical colleagues what's going on, and they can sort it out for our patients if possible. A job well done by a committed team.

So how can healing happen in a service in church? And how can I pretend to others that it does? To me healing is one of the great gifts from God, but it happens because we have been blessed with the intellect and capacity to enquire and experiment into, and ultimately understand, disease processes and, using those same God-given gifts, devise strategies and treatments to cure those afflicted. It happens in the laboratory, clinic, operating theatre and hospital ward, not in church.

And how particularly can it happen on Iona? A windswept island off another windswept island, off the windswept west coast of Scotland …

The daily rhythm of worship on Iona is balm to the soul but, oh dear, Tuesday evening is the healing service, and to make things worse – the session beforehand is on healing as well. Perhaps I should bow out and just take a walk in the unexpectantly gentle evening air and not ruin things for others. But Christ wasn't known for 'bowing out', so perhaps I'll just go and sit quietly and not interfere.

So we're all in the Chapter House, a decent crowd, many of whom I've come to know over the last few days. Our leader gets us to read the passage in which Jesus heals a paralysed man, and we talk to our neighbours about our understanding of the passage and our reaction to it. I pitch in first, cards on the table: a nice story but we now understand things like the power of suggestion and the placebo effect. But one of my neighbours says, 'But I believe it happened as the story describes, because it says so in the Bible.' I'm unnerved by the strength of my neighbour's faith but inwardly stick to my medical training guns. Soon our leader brings us back together.

Next, we are asked to respond to questions and statements that others have made in the session. A row of chairs has been put down the middle of the room, and when a question/statement is read out we have to move to one end or the other, depending on whether we agree or disagree. Goodness – why didn't I take that evening stroll?!

But the questions start and the argy-bargy and the inquisition isn't far behind. No passive sauntering to one end of the row of chairs or to the middle if you can't make up your mind. No hiding place from our leader or the others in the session. Why are you where you are on the row? What do you believe of the power of prayer and the laying on of hands to heal? Uncomfortable questions, but the space and the loving, challenging support from all is inspirational. And to hear one of the pastors in the session say, 'Everything *he* said' – after I'd had a good-going rant about not being able to pretend to people that I believed they could be cured of their physical disease by someone laying hands on them, no matter how prayerfully – was truly liberating.

We finished the session as the healing service was about to begin. Our session leader wished us well, and closed revealing that she had longstanding health problems from Crohn's disease. Now this was something I could understand, even if the exact cause of the condition is not known. I can describe in detail what it looks like down a microscope. Our leader also explained that she believed that if she was cured of Crohn's disease, for her that would be a *miracle*; while the support, understanding and love that she had received from all those who had helped her through the difficult times, that was *healing*.

Iona Abbey is a place of faith connected to God's good earth and creation, through which the oneness of God's love flows and is felt; and we, as followers of Christ, are of and one with that creation. Perhaps it is easier to feel this on Iona, and to know that we *all* have a unique place in that creation, to which we bring all the skills and talents in faith that we are given from God.

When it was time in the healing service I went up to receive the laying on of hands from a young man I did not know, and suspected would never meet again. But in that moment I also felt the loving, healing hand of God.

A sceptic healed? Yes, in many ways. Indeed the following day one of the group in the Abbey gently tapped me on the elbow as we walked in the cloisters and said that she thought a 'switch had been pressed' in me during the healing session. But perhaps most relevant to me personally is that I came to truly know that looking down that microscope day by day is to see the physical, practical healing hand of God. And most importantly, to know that by seeing this I can also see the part God wants me, uniquely, to play in the healing that is the coming of his kingdom.

David Gouldesbrough

Day 23

Living letters: from Iona to Sudan

During the time I lived and worked on Iona, two women from Sudan came to volunteer in the Abbey kitchen. They were generous, warm, amazingly life-filled people, who taught us all so much about what is truly important.

One day they expressed their need to lead a service in the Abbey. They were desperate for more people in the West to know and understand the plight of their people, and to find some help for their community back home. Sudan was in the middle of a civil war (still is …).

The worship they offered in the Abbey was a service of letters – including a letter from their minister in Sudan writing just as helicopter gunships were strafing his village; an e-mail from the volunteers back to their minister; and a letter from an aid worker sending word of the present situation, and calling for the immediate delivery of food and medicine.

After prayerfully listening to these moving letters, folk in the Abbey were invited to come to the communion table, and to join in writing a letter to the volunteers' church in Sudan.

Folk wrote simple, heartfelt messages like:

'Greetings and love from the Isle of Iona in Scotland'

'We are thinking of you'

'You are not forgotten'

'Grace to you and peace' (Thess 1:1)

'We send our love and are with you in spirit and action'

At the end of the service, the volunteers were presented with a beautiful, six-foot-long letter to take back to their village church, which several children had decorated with colourful drawings of friendly suns and rainbows, birds and flowers.

After writing the letter, folk were invited to take some campaign information away with them: leaflets focusing on a letter-writing campaign concerning the role of Western companies and corporations in civil wars in Africa.

After worship many folk expressed their desire to give some kind of offering, and so – almost the very next day – a bank account was set up in the name of the village co-operative. The co-operative sold arts and crafts, and the money earned was used to buy food for the village.

After leaving Iona the women went on a short tour of the UK, not to sight-see, but to spread wider word of the situation in their country.

Prayer

May God write a message upon your heart,
bless and direct you,
then send you out –
living letters of the Word.
Amen

Neil Paynter

Day 24

A blessing from Bethlehem

The following blessing is a rephrasing of a Christmas greeting sent in a card from Bethlehem by Hanna Azar, a Palestinian who has been a volunteer in the Abbey kitchen several times. Hanna says: *'I would love to visit this part of the world again. I have good memories of it since it was a great time with lovely people from around the world. People who shared their stories and prayers. You are always in my prayers and in my walk wherever I go, and I pray to God to bless the Community and to make it bigger to serve more people.'*

Blessing from Bethlehem

May this coming year
be full of love, joy and peace,
in our hearts, in our communities
and in our countries;
may the small Jesus Baby born in Bethlehem

light our lives,
guide our ways toward the best
and save us from all harm.

Hanna Azar

Day 23

By Clachan Corrach

My archipelago,
my long horizon,
my evening pathway
over water, to the sun:

Sheep silhouetted
on the isolated rock,
the rustle of waves,
the corncrakes' argument.

Sea smell enfolding me,
damp turf upholding me,
the iron gate swinging in memory.
On days that run

heavily, noisily,
angrily, pointlessly –
remember that Iona lies
under the same sun.

Roddy Cowie, an associate of the Iona Community

A child, bringing bread

With justice he will judge the poor
and defend the humble in the land with equity ...
The calf and the young lion will feed together,
and a little child shall lead them. (Isaiah 11:4,6)

The children walk slowly, carefully down the length of the Abbey, from sunlight through shadow, over the ancient flagstones. In their hands they are carrying bread, to give to the waiting people. This Sunday morning in Iona, the congregation's a real mixture: holidaymakers staying at different places on the island, islanders who will also go on to the Parish Church, Iona Community staff and volunteers of different ages and nationalities, and the guests who are staying in the Abbey and MacLeod Centre. This week, the Centres are full of people from urban priority areas. Some of them bear the marks of a life of deprivation or coping on the edges of an unequal society.

There are people in their Sunday best, and some with startling tattoos, folk who have been out of work for years, men who have struggled with dependency on alcohol or drugs, grandmothers who are the main carers for lively little ones, asylum seekers needing sanctuary from places of conflict: human beings with a great variety of life experience, united by this journey they've made, the shared experience of this moment.

The sermon is a challenging story about justice; the songs make all our hearts dance (the children dance too). Then, with words that are both earthy and uplifting, we come to Communion, or rather it comes to us. Representatives of this mix of humanity walk through the congregation, carrying the bread and wine. A child so small she could barely peep over the Table is now accompanied by her grandmother – but is trusted to carry the bread. The cup offered to me comes from the hands of a young boy from Sri Lanka, his father watching over him. From their vulnerability to ours, the gift of bread and wine – broken bread in a community which knows about brokenness. What happens for all of us is a moment of wholeness, hope.

Welcome to this ancient place:
house of prayer for many nations; home to all who come.
Welcome to this gathering place:
friend and stranger, saint and sinner, in all who gather here.
Come with hope or hesitation; come with joy or yearning;
all who hunger, all who thirst for life in all its fullness.
Generous God and generous Saviour, touch us through your Spirit.

(*Responses from the Sunday morning service in Iona Abbey*)

Jan Sutch Pickard, a member of the Iona Community, from Walking through Advent

Day 27

A journey and a homecoming

My journey with Iona started in a hospital ward in 2012.

I had a kidney infection, resulting in kidney failure, and a frightening two weeks. By this point I was suffering from insomnia and would scare the geriatric patients through wandering into their ward. I paced the corridors like a caged lion. One night, unable to sleep, I became aware of God's presence beside me. This time there was a very clear voice in my ear; it was the words 'go to Iona'.

When I eventually got out of hospital I knew it was only a matter of time before I would make the trip to Iona – a place I had never been before. I was 29, and had a long road ahead of me.

In the 13 months before going, I set my sights on regaining my health. I ran an average of 13 miles a week and cycled about 20. In the winter of 2012, I climbed Ben Nevis; and by January 2013 I had applied to, and been accepted by, the Iona Community to be a volunteer cook in the MacLeod Centre kitchen.

Working in the Mac kitchen changed my life! I was able to be creative, gain in confidence and make new friends. A new family in fact. We worked and talked about issues that I deeply connected with. The services in the Abbey channelled through me the love of God I had always felt. Being able to express these beliefs as well as the core message of peace and justice felt like a real homecoming. These creative, inclusive, inspirational services in the Abbey have given me energy and motivation even in the darkest moments.

Shortly before my three months as a volunteer was coming to an end, I was asked if I would like to apply for the position of Head Housekeeper in the Abbey. I jumped at the chance, and that is what I did for over a year. I fell in love with the island and the Iona Community; and before I left I got baptised in the Sound and confirmed in Bishop's House, the Episcopal retreat centre.

Also before I left, I was asked by Peter Macdonald, then Leader of the Iona Community, if I would like to join the New members programme. I was already an associate. After thinking about this for the next year, I joined the New members programme in 2015.

For my new member's project I worked at raising money and awareness for the cause of justice and peace in Israel/Palestine. This decision led me to travel to Palestine with Amos Trust to take part in the Bethlehem Half Marathon. I have memories of running past Israeli soldiers holding their guns loosely beside the Palestinian volunteers who handed me water and dates. Just as I reached the finish line, tear gas exploded behind me. I munched down on the banana being thrust into my face.

Having the opportunity to see first hand the conditions at the checkpoints and speaking to both Israeli soldiers and Palestinian civilians is an experience I will hold close to my heart forever. As I walked around a checkpoint one day I silently prayed the Iona affirmation:

With the whole church,
I affirm that we are made in God's image,
befriended by Christ,
empowered by the Spirit.

With people everywhere,
I affirm God's goodness at the heart of humanity,
planted more deeply than all that is wrong.

With all creation, I celebrate the miracle and wonder of life,
the unfolding purposes of God
forever at work in ourselves and the world.

And as I prayed, my anger and love merged, until it felt like a true energy inside me that I could draw on to help create change.

Since my visit, my hometown has helped me to host a group of young Palestinians from the Alrowwad Cultural Association/Aida Refugee Camp. It was lovely to meet them in Bethlehem – and very special to have them in Scotland.

My Iona story now comes to the time when I am just about to go to the island to be hallowed as a new member of the Iona Community, following the two-year programme.

Much has happened since getting on that bus on Mull in the spring of 2013. I will be going to the hallowing ceremony with a full heart and lots of memories. I am very grateful. Long may the Iona Community prosper.

Susan Lindsay, a member of the Iona Community

Day 28

A vision

In May 2013, I came to Iona for the first time as part of a women's retreat. My purpose in coming to the island was to provide company for my younger sister and to take pictures to use in my glass art. However, God had other plans for me, because on the last day of our trip I awoke to a vision of a large cross, with the cosmos in the centre, the words 'land, air, wind and water' on the cross arms, a goose flying overhead and a voice saying 'Iona mysteries' over and over.

I left the island knowing my life had been changed forever.

In order to try to get some clarity as to the purpose of the vision, I signed up for a second retreat in May 2014.

On my first morning back on Iona, I woke up very early, grabbed my camera and walked down to the boathouse and stood watching the sunrise, the water and the gulls, praying to God for clarity as to what God wanted of me. Then, all of a sudden, the gulls flew off and it grew very quiet. Out of the corner of my eye I noticed one large gull flying low towards me around the corner of the boathouse, but as it got closer, I could see it was a goose and, as I was taking a photo of it, I heard a voice say, 'Follow the Wild Goose.'

I found the guidance to allow the Holy Spirit to enter my life then. Had I never come to Iona I might never have opened my mind long enough to hear God's calling.

Lesley Kelly

Day 29

A launch pad for earthy engagement

'So you're off to Iona again. On retreat, I suppose?'

Well, actually, no. Whatever else Iona is, a retreat it is not – at least not in the way the word is normally understood. Iona is not a place of escape, but somewhere to renew commitment to God's world. The wisdom of Iona points to an engaged spirituality.

Part of the clue lies in its origins. It is a mistaken assumption that when Columba left Ireland in 563, he was abandoning forever the world of power politics.

He was certainly present at the Convention of Drum Cett (near Limavady, N. Ireland) in 575, and was in all probability a major player in that great gathering, which negotiated the royal succession – and according to some historians established peace in the region for fifty years.

What Columba left behind when he quit Ireland was the use of violence in the pursuit of political power. As an 'island soldier' he was aligning himself with a different kind of power – a power to heal, reconcile and make peace. In the same way, Cuthbert, wrestling with his demons on the Inner Farne, facing Bamburgh across the water, was a living reminder to the king in his royal stronghold of a higher power to which he was ultimately answerable.

In our own time, the Trappist monk Thomas Merton, living an apparently disengaged life at Gethsemani in the remote Kentucky countryside, was, in his prayer, fully engaged with the world; through his writings he informed and inspired a whole generation of social and political activists.

Once when preparing to return home from some days on Iona I wrote the following:

It's always hard to leave.

Iona:
this thin place of sharp
remembering.
But necessary.
Iona is not a terminus, but a stage on
a larger journey,
a launch pad
for earthy engagement.

Prayer

Lord, teach us when we are inclined to forget,
that places of retreat are not places of escape;
that when we clasp hands in prayer
we take responsibility with you for your world;
that worship and politics
are not separate in your economy,
nor should they be in ours.
Because it was your Son who taught us
to pray for your Kingdom to come
in the here and now,
in this place and time:

for your will to be done on earth
as in heaven.
We dare to pray in his name.
Amen

Warren Bardsley, a member of the Iona Community, from Gathered and Scattered

Day 30

Steps

When you live on an island
everything happens
somewhere else, they say.
These small dancing steps
on the sand
to the rhythm of sea
and music of wind
are a story waiting to begin
in another place.
Now, as far inland
as it is possible
to be, I can't pick out
the steps you taught us
then, or bring to mind
the name of the dance
the four of us did,
on the beach.
But I remember the pattern,
the weaving and threading
the shape and sharing

of a turning point.
I remember hands held out
and hands clasped;
I remember, against a greying sky,
dancing
into the sun again.

Joy Mead, a member of the Iona Community, from Lent and Easter Readings from Iona

Day 31

A story from the road

When I left Iona after Easter week, I wondered if I'd ever meet Jesus again – in the 'real world'.

The week had been so powerful for me. The coming together of so many things in my time on Iona. In my life. Sitting in the cloisters and crying after the Maundy Thursday service – after Jesus was arrested, and the communion table was stripped and draped in black. The waiting in desolation and depression. And then, on Easter Sunday – Resurrection. Lighting candles at midnight and singing 'Christ be our Light'. Hugging everyone.

Iona, for me, was a place where I finally started to face the issues in my life. Issues like abandonment, betrayal, death … I started seeing patterns in my life, and in the life of the world. I began seeing how Jesus' story was, as they say, 'a story to live by'. Christ started to live in me. In my flesh and blood.

I was feeling down when I left the island, emotional – I hadn't felt that emotional in a long time. A real grief: leaving community and all we had shared living and working together. I felt wrung out, but hopeful. Vulnerable, but open.

I left with a group; we shared a meal on the ferry to Oban – bread and cheese and a thermos of tea – and did the morning office together. Then, gradually, we all went our separate ways: out into the world. All the witnesses – dispersed. We would keep in touch, we said. Write letters.

I had some tough times, some dead ends it seemed like. But I tried to remain hopeful and disciplined. Then it started to happen: I visited a man I knew who was living in a nursing home. He was talking to me. About his life. He'd had a stroke. He was writing everything down so that he could remember, he said – the names of things and the people who came to visit him. Still, life was good: he enjoyed the music appreciation and poetry evenings they had at the home, the good food. The view out back of the pine and cedar trees – evergreen scent with the windows wide and curtains dancing.

He was thankful, he told me, and smiled. It wasn't easy for him to smile: he'd lost control of the muscles all down one side of his face, all down one side of his heavy body. I was thinking to myself that it was pretty amazing – him smiling – and then, all of a sudden, in a flash, I recognised him as the Christ: Christ on the cross. Christ, resurrected. He asked me about my time on Iona.

Talking to him, sitting with him there, healed me in a way.

I visited my folks. We had grown closer somehow. My mother told me things I never knew about her, things she had gone through growing up. She was telling me a story, and suddenly the lines in her face in the soft, late evening light were beautiful: there was an agony in the garden traced there; but a sign of the Resurrection somehow, too.

Then I met a homeless man in London, in Euston station. We were talking intensely: about life, about suffering. But about how wonderful and mysterious and incredible life is, too. We shared his bottle and my fish and chips. He had a very profound understanding – well, he'd been through a lot in his life. A lot of abandonment, betrayal, death … Every day I guess: waking up in the park, walking down the road into the city to be crucified by the state, by the crowds, by his self.

We were very honest with each other. He shared a poem he'd written; recited it by heart with his eyes closed. I started to cry, it was so beautiful. I can't say what it was about, exactly. It was the way he spoke and sang it. Something in his broken, scarred voice. In his transfigured, life-lined face. It was like the poem was light and resurrection above all the pain and suffering – all the pain and suffering in the world. I turned to thank him but he had gone, disappeared. I saw him later, walking ahead of me; shuffling and stumbling through the crowd at King's Cross station.

Sometimes I recognise Christ in moments like that. Other times, it's more in the everyday: sharing good news or lunch with a friend; turning and meeting a stranger's smile; in company of a partner as we journey along, or pause somewhere in the heart of silence – moments like that. I try to remain open to it. It's not always easy.

'Greetings,' I wrote to my Iona friend. 'Christ is risen! So, have you seen him?'

He responded, on a postcard of a city sunrise: 'Christ is risen! He is risen indeed!'

He's doing volunteer work. I'm getting ideas of going back to school – nursing maybe? Terry is working midnights at a corner shop in Sheffield: it's not the job, he says, it's the people. The people who come in off the cold, mean streets; talking to them at all hours. Listening. If he can just learn to stay open, he says.

Julie is travelling. Last time Ray heard she was somewhere in South India. I still feel we're all connected. Who knows, maybe we'll meet again one day.

I have moments sometimes when I can see light radiating and glancing off everything, everyone. It's like the light I witnessed on Iona: that beautiful, warm, amazing light falling, like God's glowing grace, on the Ross of Mull; shining on the sea.

They say that Iona is 'a thin place': a place where the separation between the material and the spiritual realm is only tissue-thin. It's tissue-thin everywhere I'm discovering: in India; in Euston station; in hometowns; in lonely, desperate corner shops at drunken midnight ... Everywhere, I want to cry, and shout, 'Hallelujah – yes!'

Neil Paynter

Sources

A Pilgrim's Guide to Iona Abbey, Chris Polhill, Wild Goose Publications, 2006

A Way of Knowing, Joy Mead, Wild Goose Publications, 2012

Advent Readings from Iona, Jan Sutch Pickard and Brian Woodcock, Wild Goose Publications, 2005

An Iona Prayer Book, Peter Millar, Canterbury Press, 1998

Around a Thin Place: An Iona Pilgrimage Guide, by Jane Bentley and Neil Paynter, Wild Goose Publications, 2011

Bare Feet and Buttercups: Resources for Ordinary Time, Ruth Burgess, Wild Goose Publications, 2008

Chasing the Wild Goose: the Story of the Iona Community, Ron Ferguson, Wild Goose Publications, reprinted 2000

Christ of the Celts: The Healing of Creation, J. Philip Newell, Wild Goose Publications, 2009

Coracle: the magazine of the Iona Community, Neil Paynter (Ed.), and others

Fire and Bread: Resources for Eastertide, by Ruth Burgess, Wild Goose Publications, 2007

Gathered and Scattered: Readings and Meditations from the Iona Community, Neil Paynter (Ed.), Wild Goose Publications, 2007

Good News of Great Joy: Daily Readings for Advent from Around the World, Neil Paynter and Peter Millar, Wild Goose Publications, 2013

Hay and Stardust: Resources for Christmas to Candlemas, Ruth Burgess, Wild Goose Publications, 2005

Holy Ground: Liturgies and Worship Resources for an Engaged Spirituality, Helen Boothroyd and Neil Paynter, Wild Goose Publications, 2005

In the Gift of this New Day: Praying with the Iona Community, Neil Paynter (Ed.), Wild Goose Publications, 2016

Invisible We See You: Tracing Celtic Threads Through Christian Community, Nancy Cocks, Wild Goose Publications, 2006

Iona Dawn: Through Holy Week with the Iona Community, Neil Paynter, Wild Goose Publications, 2006

Iona: God's Energy: The Vision and Spirituality of the Iona Community, Norman Shanks, Wild Goose Publications, reprinted 2009

Iona: Images and Reflections, David Coleman and Neil Paynter, Wild Goose Publications, 2007

Jesus' Healing Works and Ours, Ian Cowie, Wild Goose Publications, 2000

Lent and Easter Readings from Iona, Neil Paynter, Wild Goose Publications, 2004

No Extraordinary Power: Prayer, Stillness and Activism, Helen Steven, Quaker Books, 2005

Out of Iona: Words from a Crossroads of the World, Jan Sutch Pickard, Wild Goose Publications, 2006

The Green Heart of the Snowdrop, Kate McIlhagga, Wild Goose Publications, 2004

This Is the Day: Readings and Meditations from the Iona Community, Neil Paynter, Wild Goose Publications, 2007

Walking through Advent: Daily Readings, Jan Sutch Pickard, Wild Goose Publications, 2014

Some Iona resources

Adomnán's 'Law of the Innocents' – Cain Adomnán: A Seventh-century Law for the Protection of Non-Combatants, Gilbert Márkus, Kilmartin Museum, 2008

Against the Tide: The Story of Adomnán of Iona, Warren Bardsley, Wild Goose Publications, 2006

An Iona Anthology, F. Marian McNeill, New Iona Press, 1990

An Iona Prayer Book, Peter Millar, Canterbury Press, 1998

Around a Thin Place: An Iona Pilgrim Guide, Jane Bentley and Neil Paynter, Wild Goose Publications, 2011

A Wee Book of Iona Poems, Kenneth Steven, Wild Goose Publications, 2015

Chasing the Wild Goose: the Story of the Iona Community, Ron Ferguson, Wild Goose Publications, reprinted 2000

Columba's Iona: A New History, Rosalind K. Marshall, Sandstone Press Ltd, 2014

Columba's Island: Iona from Past to Present, E. Mairi MacArthur, Edinburgh University Press, 1995

Eternity Dipping into Time, Kathy Galloway, Wild Goose Publications (download), 2012

Flowers of Iona, Jean M. Millar, New Iona Press, 1993

Inventory of the Ancient Monuments: Argyll Vol. 4, Royal Commission on the Ancient and Historical Monuments of Scotland, 1982

Iona, Anna Ritchie, Historic Scotland/Batsford, 1997

Iona (Colin Baxter Island Guides), E. Mairi MacArthur and Iain Sarjeant, Colin Baxter, 2001

Iona Abbey Worship Book, Wild Goose Publications, new edition 2017

Iona: A Map, Wild Goose Publications, new edition, 2017

Iona and Staffa (DVD), script by E. Mairi MacArthur, Video Highland Productions, 2001

Iona Celtic Art: The Work of Alexander and Euphemia Ritchie, New Iona Press, 2003

Iona: Dove across the Water (film), director, Mike Alexander, Films of Scotland (see the Scottish Screen Archive website)

Iona: God's Energy: The Vision and Spirituality of the Iona Community, Norman Shanks, Wild Goose Publications, reprinted 2009

Iona: Images and Reflections, David Coleman and Neil Paynter, Wild Goose Publications, 2007

Iona: Pilgrim Guide, Peter Millar, illustrations by Gordon Menzies, Canterbury Press, 1997

Iona Portrayed: The Island through Artists' Eyes 1790-1960, Jessica Christian and Charles Stiller, New Iona Press, 2000

Iona, Staffa and Ross of Mull Ordnance Survey Explorer Map, Ordnance Survey, 2007

Iona: The Earliest Poetry of a Celtic Monastery, Thomas Owen Clancy and Gilbert Márkus, Edinburgh University Press, 1995

Iona: The Living Memory of a Crofting Community, E. Mairi MacArthur, Polygon, 1990

Life of St Columba (trans. Richard Sharpe), Adomnán of Iona, Penguin Classics, 2005

Out of Iona: Words from a Crossroads of the World, Jan Sutch Pickard, Wild Goose Publications, 2016

That Illustrious Island: Iona through Travellers' Eyes, E. Mairi MacArthur (ed.), New Iona Press, 1991

The Cloisters of Iona Abbey, Ewan Mathers, Wild Goose Publications, new edition 2017

The Iona Community: Today's Hope, Tomorrow's Challenge/Sermon in Stone (DVD), Wild Goose Publications, 1998

The Isle of Iona: Sacred, Spectacular, Living, Alastair De Watteville, 1998

The Story of Iona: An Illustrated History and Guide, Rosemary Power, Canterbury Press, 2013

The Whole Earth Shall Cry Glory: Iona Prayers, George MacLeod, Wild Goose Publications, reprinted 2016